COMMA SENSE

COMMA
SENSE

Praise for *Comma Sense*

"I first learned of Ellen Feld's impeccable command of all things grammatical when she was one of the wisest hires I ever made as the editor-in-chief of a business newspaper in New York City. More than three decades later I am thrilled—and yes, even still enlightened—to read her guide to the grammatical arts. I am, as well, delightedly entertained by her in the process. *Comma Sense* (the artfulness of that pun cum apt observation is typical of her) is a downright treasure of a book for all who write, read, or speak the English language."

—**ROBERT OLEN BUTLER**, author of the Pulitzer Prize-winning *A Good Scent from a Strange Mountain*

"Writing a simple memo is essential to success in the business world. So it's astonishing how many college and professional school graduates can't structure a simple sentence. As someone who's corrected many a colleague's work, I fervently hope Ellen Feld's easy-to-read book will sit on many office desks. Its clear style and simple format make it an excellent reference. But I also hope that some enterprising grade school teachers will assign this to their classes. It's so accessible, it could be an antidote to the American epidemic of graduating students who can't write."

—**DANA MILLER ERVIN**, former journalist for ABC and CBS News

"If you really want to go deep into the 'how' and 'why' of grammar, then *Comma Sense* is for you. Ellen covers the basics like a pro and delivers practical examples to help you learn. You'll never mess up 'lie' and 'lay' again!"

—**LISA LEPKI**, CMO at ProWritingAid

"Sadly neglected in public school education, grammar has become something that's winged even by the most educated. What's needed is a guidebook, and Ellen Feld has given us one, written by a writer, educator, and editor who knows the rules and communicates them with panache and an exemplary prose style. You'll actually enjoy learning English grammar while reading *Comma Sense*. And you may pick up a little something extra along the way."

—**RICK MULLIN**, senior editor of *Chemical & Engineering News*

"If you're going to have one grammar book on your shelf, make it this one! Ellen's explanations are clear, concise, and will get you writing or revising with confidence and zeal."

—**DANI ALCORN**, COO at Writing Academy and cofounder of Writer's Secret Sauce

"Everything you need to know about grammar in less than 300 pages! If you write for a living, have dreams of becoming a proofreader, or just want to enhance your communication skills, *Comma Sense* is the book for you. As an editor, I've read countless grammar books, but *Comma Sense* is hands down my favorite. Ellen's book is full of fun, easy-to-understand examples and quizzes to test what you've learned. Who doesn't love a quiz? Don't let this book out of your sight, because you're going to want to have it just within reach whenever you have a tricky grammar question!"

—**CATHERINE TURNER**, editor and owner of Turner Proofreading

"In her new book, *Comma Sense*, Ellen Sue Feld demystifies grammar with clarity, conciseness, and empathy."

—**ANU GARG**, author and founder of Wordsmith.org

COMMA SENSE

Your Guide to
Grammar Victory

Ellen Sue Feld

TURNER

PUBLISHING COMPANY

Turner Publishing Company
Nashville, Tennessee
www.turnerpublishing.com

Cover & Layout Design: Carmen Fortunato
Author photo by Jo Rosen Photography/Johanna Resnick Rosen

Library of Congress Cataloging-in-Publication number: 2021946716
ISBN: (print) 978-1-64250-725-6, (ebook) 978-1-64250-726-3
BISAC category code LAN006000, LANGUAGE ARTS & DISCIPLINES / Grammar
& Punctuation

Printed in the United States of America

TABLE OF CONTENTS

To everyone who asked, asks, and will ask questions—

I've had the pleasure of meeting thousands of people through teaching grammar—from middle schoolers to octogenarians—some in the face-to-face classroom, most online.

Sometimes, people feel self-conscious about what they don't know. For them it can be an act of bravery to ask a question, exposing themselves to other people's judgment.

Their questions inspire me to keep on learning and to share what I know, which in turn, I hope, will inspire them.

TABLE OF CONTENTS

INTRODUCTION

Welcome to *Comma Sense: Your Guide to Grammar Victory*!

Before we jump into our first grammar topic, I'd like to say hello and tell you why I've written this book for you. Hello! I'm Ellen Sue Feld, and I wrote *Comma Sense* after nearly twenty years of creating and teaching online grammar courses. Before and during some of that time, I also taught college English courses.

As a subject, grammar is always in fashion because we all need to use it, but the imperative to teach it hasn't always run side by side with that need. Lots of us never got much of a grammar education, and this is true even for people with advanced degrees.

I came at grammar through the side door to my first teaching job. I suddenly found myself unprepared in a classroom full of students who'd tested into a course they were required to take before English composition. Their first stack of intimidating papers (and they were *paper* then) was the catalyst for my interest in teaching grammar. I had no idea how to comment constructively on their essays.

I didn't have a grammar language to share with students, so I started studying their textbook. Then I made grammar part of the way we worked on refining writing. And that's what I'm still doing now, some forty years later.

I've never believed writing is all about grammar. It's not. Good grammar doesn't make good writing, but good writing demands good grammar.

Let's explore why you're here.

All kinds of writing ask us to use our grammar smarts, and most of us have to do some kind of writing, whoever we are, whatever we do. We have applications to fill out and forms to complete. We have to email bosses, patients, staff, teachers, government officials, family, or friends. We all want and need to be understood.

Our writing represents who we are.

The goal of this book is to help you accomplish any kind of writing without second-guessing yourself. You'll learn where to put a comma, what to capitalize, and lots more.

This book is for everyone. We're all communicators.

Grammar is full of rules. Those rules are like a recipe we can follow so we can be sure to create exactly the dish we had in mind, even if we're not master chefs. *Comma Sense* will give you the rules (or recipes) of grammar, whether you were never exposed to them, you knew them and forgot them, you were confused by them, or you were maybe taking a little snooze back in Mr. Gray's ninth-grade English class.

Some people love having rules to follow. But if you're a nonconformist and don't like rules, no worries! Once you know the rules, you can decide to use them when you need to or break them with skill and insight.

You'll learn what you need to know to include good grammar in everything you write. You'll be able to do it with more confidence, and having that ability will feel great!

By the way, language is alive, and its rules change through the decades. Though most of the rules we'll talk about are steadfast, others are flexible, and some may even die.

Throughout the book, I refer to writing, but you'll find that much of what you learn here applies to speaking too.

Here's something great about learning grammar: You get to practice your new skills every time you communicate, and the more you do it, the more seamlessly good grammar will blend into your writing.

Because the topics here build sequentially, you'll find it most useful to read the chapters in order. But backtrack anytime you need to! Real learning often involves retracing our steps and then stepping forward again. Each chapter has a quiz at the end to help you put your newfound skills to the test. Please choose one best answer for each question.

A note about typographical conventions you'll see throughout the book:

- italics = to show a word used as a *word*
- underline = to <u>highlight</u> words
- boldface = to **emphasize** words, often in relationship to underlined words

Let's get started!

THE GREAT EIGHT

(parts of speech)

Introduction

Uh-oh. Here we go. Terms! Why do you need to know the names for things? The very idea of terms has alienated many a would-be grammarian. But not here and now!

Once you reframe the idea of terms, you'll feel good about using them. Terms are great because they give us a way to talk about grammar. They provide a shared vocabulary for you and me so that we can understand each other. They give us a grammar *lexicon*. A lexicon is a vocabulary that's specific to a group or subject. Grammar has its own lexicon.

You're about to meet the eight parts of speech. If you've met them before, that's okay. Sometimes we need to be reintroduced to get really familiar and comfortable with a topic.

You've probably heard about pronouns and conjunctions and prepositions and interjections, but do you have a clear idea of what they are? What's an adverb, anyway? You'll find out in this chapter as you begin to identify the different parts of speech and see how they fit together to make a sentence.

Lesson 1: Verbs, Nouns, and Pronouns

Right now, you're going to get familiar with the different kinds of words you may meet in a sentence. One of your goals, after all, is to be able to write a beautiful sentence. And by beautiful, I mean grammatical!

Meet one of your grammar avatars: Aunt Felicity. She's a pro at baking. (You love her famous sugar cookies.) She's going to bake some cookies now. And while she does, we're going to assist her by adding our own ingredients—parts of speech—to make a sentence.

Our first ingredient is verbs.

Verbs

verb: **bake**

Verbs are what we do or think or are.

There are two basic verb types: action verbs and linking verbs.

1. Action Verbs

Don't let the word action fool you. Some actions are extremely physical—such as *climb or wrestle*—while others are quiet or sedentary—like *nap or imagine*. But even if you're napping, you're doing something. You're engaged in an action.

More examples of action verbs are:

- drive
- energize
- run
- shop
- think
- wish
- yodel

2. Linking Verbs

Linking verbs do what their name indicates: They create a link. In mathematics, we have the equal sign. In grammar, we have linking verbs. In a sentence, they equate—or connect—what's on their left to what's on their right.

> Mr. Gray <u>was</u> a strict grammarian.

> Aunt Felicity <u>seems</u> happy all the time.

Many linking verbs come from the verbs *be*, *become*, and *seem*. Here are examples:

- am
- became
- is

- seemed
- was

Other linking verbs are related to our five senses: sight, smell, hearing, taste, and touch.

Here are a few examples of those:

- feel
- smell
- taste

They're a funny group, however, because sometimes these verbs work as linking verbs and sometimes as action verbs. Their function depends on context.

> Those cookies <u>smell</u> sweet. (*Smell* is a linking verb, as in cookies = sweet.)

> The bloodhound <u>smells</u> the assailant's sock before tracking begins. (*Smells* is an action verb, as in the bloodhound is doing something.)

The idea of function will be with us throughout the book.

Some words work only as one part of speech. Others can work as multiple parts of speech. Their function in a sentence determines which part.

For example, some of the verbs on the list of action verbs, like *run* and *wish*, are also nouns, and that's our next part of speech.

Nouns

noun: **aunt**

Nouns are names for people, places, things, or ideas:

- person: aunt
- place: store
- thing: food
- idea: wisdom

All of these are *common nouns*. Most nouns are common nouns.

We also have *proper nouns*, meaning they're special (and sometimes unique) names for people, places, things, and ideas. We capitalize proper nouns:

- person: <u>Felicity</u> begins with an uppercase letter.
- place: <u>Wyoming</u> begins with an uppercase letter.
- thing: <u>Fitbit</u> begins with an uppercase letter.
- idea: <u>Murphy's Law</u> begins with an uppercase letter *M* and an uppercase letter *L*.

Nouns are the words we use to identify things. Without nouns, we might run around all our lives like toddlers asking, "What's this? What's that?"

Believe it or not, you already have the ingredients for a grammatical sentence. You can add a noun to a verb and make a complete sentence: Aunt Felicity bakes.

Pronouns

pronoun: **she**

We can use a pronoun instead of a noun to partner with our verb.

First, we might say:

> Aunt Felicity bakes.

Next, we can use a pronoun to refer to Aunt Felicity:

> <u>She</u> bakes.

Or we can ask:

> <u>Who</u> bakes?

A pronoun and a verb can make a complete sentence. Pronouns step in—or substitute—for nouns. They add a little variety, and they offer some relief from the monotony of repeating a noun.

Compare these two sentences:

> Aunt Felicity is a great baker, and Aunt Felicity sends her family cookies every month.

> Aunt Felicity is a great baker, and <u>she</u> sends her family cookies every month.

Even though we love Aunt Felicity, once in a sentence is probably enough to see her name.

Here are some more examples of pronouns:

- all
- each
- he
- I
- it
- one
- somebody
- that
- which

You've just reviewed three parts of speech: verb, noun, and pronoun. And you've made a few grammatical sentences.

Lesson 2: Adjectives and Adverbs

Now that you've met verbs and nouns, let's look at words that tell us more about them.

Adjectives

adjective: **energetic**

Adjective in a sentence: <u>Energetic</u> Aunt Felicity bakes.

What kind of person is Aunt Felicity? <u>Energetic</u>! That's why she bakes so many cookies!

Adjectives tell us about nouns. They modify nouns, which means they give further definition to nouns. Here are some examples of adjectives:

- angry
- nice
- tall
- ravenous

The three little words *a*, *an*, and *the* are *articles*. Articles are a kind of adjective.

We use *the* when we're being specific:

> He'd like <u>the</u> reddest apple in the bowl because he thinks it looks like <u>the</u> juiciest one.

The words *the*, *reddest*, and *juiciest* are all adjectives modifying *apple*. They tell us more about it.

We use *a* or *an* when we're not being specific:

> Would your friend like <u>a</u> piece of fruit? Sure, he'd love <u>an</u> apple. He's happy to have any old apple.

Why do we use *a* versus *an*?

We use *a* before words that begin with a hard sound, usually a consonant.

- a cake
- a plate
- a yellow lemon

We use *an* before soft sounds, usually a vowel:

- an excellent idea
- an icon
- an octopus

As we choose between *a* and *an*, we may need to pay attention to how we'd read something aloud versus how it appears on the page.

Sometimes a vowel has a hard sound like a consonant does, and then we precede it with *a*:

- a unicorn
- a eulogy

Sometimes a consonant is pronounced like a vowel, and then we use *an*:

- an MFA degree
  We pronounce consonant "M" as "em" when we read aloud.
- an FDA approval
  We pronounce consonant "F" as "ef" when we read aloud.

When you're not sure which article to use, switch from silent reading to saying the words aloud. That will guide you to the right choice.

Adverbs

adverb: **efficiently**

Adverb in a sentence: Energetic Aunt Felicity bakes <u>efficiently</u>.

What do adverbs do? They do for verbs what adjectives do for nouns. Adverbs are words that give further definition to—or modify—verbs. They also modify adjectives and other adverbs. They give answers to the questions how, when, where, and to what extent.

How does Aunt Felicity bake? <u>Efficiently</u>!
    Here are a few adverbs:

- apparently
- terribly
- well

Many adverbs end in *ly*. Knowing this helps us identify them. Here are examples of adverbs at work:

- Modifying a verb: Energetic Aunt Felicity bakes <u>early</u>.
- Modifying another adverb: She bakes <u>quite</u> early.
- Modifying an adjective: <u>Surprisingly</u> energetic Aunt Felicity bakes.

Now you know that adjectives and adverbs are modifiers.

Lesson 3: Conjunctions, Prepositions, and Interjections

You have three more parts of speech to meet.

Conjunctions

conjunction: **and**

Conjunction in a sentence: Energetic Aunt Felicity bakes efficiently <u>and</u> sweetly.

Conjunctions are connectors. We'll look at more conjunctions down the road. For now, let's start with the basic group called the *coordinating conjunctions*:

- for
- and
- nor
- but
- or
- yet
- so

Listed this way, the coordinating conjunctions create the tried-and-true acronym FANBOYS. When you think of it, you'll be able to recall them. Each letter in the acronym stands for the first letter of a coordinating conjunction on the list.

Their name *coordinating* makes their function easy to remember because the prefix *co* means *joint* or *together*. Conjunctions can join anything from a single word to another single word, like a noun to a noun, to a long, complicated thought to another long, complicated thought.

We'll revisit them and other conjunctions in upcoming lessons.

Here are a few sentences that use coordinating conjunctions:

Dad <u>and</u> Mom shop.

Dad can peel, <u>but</u> Mom can slice <u>and</u> dice!

Mom <u>and</u> Dad work well together in the kitchen, <u>for</u> they have been a team for thirty-two years.

Prepositions

preposition: **in**

Preposition in a sentence: Energetic Aunt Felicity bakes efficiently and sweetly <u>in</u> the kitchen.

Prepositions are a kind of locator. They create a relationship between a noun or pronoun and someone or something else in a sentence. This relationship may be based on place, time, movement, or function.

The preposition *in* places Aunt Felicity somewhere: the kitchen.

More examples of prepositions are:

- above
- at
- to
- with

Some prepositions are more than one word:

- according to
- as for
- next to

Prepositions raise another grammar topic: *idioms*.

What's an idiom? It's an established group of words that together create an expression whose meaning differs from the literal meaning of the words, like "What's up?"

If we tried to translate the words into another language, they wouldn't make a whole lot of sense. However, we understand the idiom to mean any of the following: What are you doing? What's happening in your life? What do you want? Do you have something to tell me? Can I do something for you?

In English, we use many prepositions idiomatically, by partnering them with another word or word group. Here are some examples:

- based on
- familiar with
- similar to

These idioms can be tricky for all of us and particularly for those of you whose first language isn't English. The good news is that you can look up idioms in a resource like an online idiom dictionary. (Visit the Resources section toward the end of the book.)

Interjections

interjection: **wow**

Interjection in a sentence: <u>Wow</u>, energetic Aunt Felicity bakes efficiently and sweetly in the kitchen.

Ta-da! You're on the eighth part of speech already!

Interjections just might be the most fun of all. We don't have to worry too much about them. They add a little spice and emphasis to our writing. They are, however, typically very casual, so we use them in informal writing and more liberally in speaking than in writing.

Interjections are words or short phrases that have a shout or a punch to them. More examples of interjections are:

- good grief
- hey
- no
- whew

An interjection can stand as a "sentence" unto itself. You'll sometimes see one before or after a full sentence, standing alone, followed by a punctuation mark:

- It was great seeing you. Bye.
- Hey! Stop that.

Now What?

Okay, you've just met the eight parts of speech: verb, noun, pronoun, adjective, adverb, conjunction, preposition, and interjection.

You might be thrilled because you're thinking, "Oh, yeah. This is coming back to me. I remember those adjectives and adverbs."

Or you might be thinking, "So what? Why do I need to know all this? What's the point?"

Think *sugar cookie!*

By that I mean: Think *grammatical sentence.*

Here's what you could do with your new or refreshed parts-of-speech know-how.

You're at a baseball game. It's a close game at the bottom of the ninth inning. The first batter strikes out. Through the booing, you hear a spectator next to you say, "He swung the bat terrible."

Wait a minute, you think, the word *swung* is a verb, and the word *terrible* tells us how the batter swung, but *terrible* is an adjective. The word should be *terribly*! That's an adverb. We use an adverb, not an adjective, to modify a verb.

I hope you're not going to say a word to the spectator. Not everyone in every venue is as excited about grammar as you and I are right now. And you certainly don't need to start naming every part of speech you see in every sentence.

But the next time you write a sentence, you'll know what kind of word to use when you want to modify your verb. How do you want to write? You want to write *well*! You don't want to write *good*. You want to write *well*. Why? Because *good* is an adjective, *well* is an adverb, and you need an adverb to modify your verb *write*.

That's one small example of how understanding parts of speech can make your writing better.

Lesson 4: You and Your Dictionary

Before we wrap up this first chapter, I'm going to steer you toward one of the best resources ever: your dictionary.

You're probably acquainted with using a dictionary to check spelling. Your dictionary can do a lot more for you. It can answer grammar questions, including questions about parts of speech.

As a kid, I got so frustrated when I'd ask my mom and dad how to spell something and they'd answer, "Look it up." How annoying! If I already knew how to spell it, I wouldn't need to look it up, and I wouldn't have asked for help in the first place. This calls for an interjection: Argh!

We've come a long way from the days of having only print dictionaries. (I still have mine, I still love them, and I still recommend you get one too.) There are so many terrific resources at your fingertips. Online dictionaries can be a tremendous help because as you begin to type a word, spelling suggestions sometimes magically appear. Along the way, you'll find yourself interested in some words you didn't know existed. (It's easy to have fun getting lost in a dictionary.)

Once you find your word, you'll see its spelling and its identification by part of speech. This is fantastic! I'll save more of my dictionary talk for later in the book. You'll get tired of me, but truly, I can't oversell this grammar tool.

IN A NUTSHELL

Congratulations! You can now identify the eight basic parts of speech:

- verb
- noun
- pronoun
- adjective
- adverb
- conjunction
- preposition
- interjection

Only two are required to make a sentence: a noun and a verb, or a pronoun and a verb.

Sometimes an interjection stands alone as a "sentence," but this is best for informal writing.

You've also begun to develop a grammar lexicon. And your dictionary will help you explore that lexicon.

If you look at one of those eight parts of speech all by itself, it might seem like an insignificant ingredient. But put a few of those ingredients together in just the right combination, and you'll have a sugar cookie—or a beautiful sentence.

Of course, sugar cookies alone don't make a complete or satisfying meal. There's a lot more to our grammar menu coming up!

FAQs

Q: How do I know what part of speech a word is?

A: First, try using the word in a sentence. When you look at a word in relationship to other words in a sentence, you may recognize what part of speech it is.

Second, you'll find your dictionary is a great resource. When a word can work as multiple parts of speech, a dictionary will list an entry for each, often offering sentence examples so that you can see the word in operation.

Q: Can you give an example of a linking verb that's also an action verb?

A: Yes, the verb *feel* is an example.

"I feel pretty good today!" In that sentence, *feel* is a linking verb that's equating *I* and *good*.

"My fingers feel the tiny stitches of the fabric." In that sentence, *feel* is an action verb. Its meaning is similar to *examine*.

Q: Are there more than eight parts of speech?

A: Some grammar guides consider articles and/or determiners (words like *one*, *that*, or *my*) to be discrete categories, bringing the total to nine or ten parts of speech. In this book, we talk about eight because we think of articles and determiners as part of the adjective group.

Chapter 1 Quiz

Question 1

Which two parts of speech can create a complete sentence without any additional words?

    a. adjective and verb

    b. noun and adverb

    c. pronoun and verb

Question 2

Identify a preposition in the following sentence: "Do you have a jar of sunflower seed butter in the fridge?"

    a. of

    b. butter

    c. do

Question 3

Which article would precede *UFO*?

    a. a

    b. an

    c. either one

Answer Key: Q1:c Q2:a Q3:a

WHICH WITCH IS WHICH?

(mixed-up words)

Introduction

KEYWORDS:

◊ homophone

◊ possessive pronoun

◊ contraction

Advice/advise, lay/lie, passed/past, their/there. It's easy to confuse and misuse words like these. Have you ever found yourself wondering which word to use? Today, you're going to learn about mixed-up words. What are they? They're words we incorrectly use in place of other words.

Are you familiar with an aha moment that arrives a few seconds too late? Proudly, you send off a piece of writing, sit back to enjoy reviewing what you wrote, and then suddenly discover a blooper. Did you tell a coworker about what you learned in the previous grammar *lessen*? Oops! You meant grammar *lesson*.

When we write, it's easy to key in the wrong word, especially if we're tired or multitasking. But we can train ourselves to spot mistakes. And if we can spot them, we can fix them.

We'll take a look at three groups of mixed-up words. Then you'll learn some techniques for choosing the right one from each pair or triplet of mix-ups.

By the time you finish Chapter 2, you'll be *paring pears* for fruit salad and *setting* aside the *peels* for another *purpose*, instead of *pairing pairs* and *sitting* aside *peals* for another *porpoise*!

Lesson 1: Homophones

We're going to start with homophones, so let's give definition to the word: *Hom* means "same," and *phone* means "sound." You may have guessed that homophones have the same sound. Yes, homophones are words that sound alike. No wonder we often mix up words like the infamous *principal/principle* duo or the *to/too/two* triad. Homophones share a sound, but they don't share a meaning.

Homophones typically come in pairs or triplets, like *days/daze* or *cite/sight/site*.

I'm going to try to whe*t* (not *wet*, right?) your appetite for learning more about homophones with the following scenario.

Let's say your birthday's coming up, and you want to do something special. You've decided to throw yourself a small dinner party. You've decided to go all out and send printed invitations!

You want a snazzy, formal party. (If this isn't your style, don't worry. We're using this imaginary scenario to learn about words, not parties.) You choose classic stationery (not *stationary*), and because you don't want to hire a professional calligrapher, you find an elegant font and create a stunning invitation to mail (not *male*) to your prospective (not *perspective*) guests.

Your invitation begins this way: "The honor of your presents is requested at my dinner party."

That hits the right tone for your party and sounds good, right? Or does it?

Simple mistakes can lead to big gaps in meaning. In this case, you wrote *presents* instead of *presence*. Chances are, everyone will understand your invitation. Your friends know you're inviting them, not their gifts, to dinner. But let's figure out how to make sure you write what you intend. You want to write what's right!

Why do we mistake words for each other? It's easy for our brains to get confused when words with different spellings and meanings sound alike.

When someone speaks the word *through*, it sounds exactly the same as *threw*. When you're writing late at night, or you haven't had enough sleep, or you're not giving your full attention to your writing process, you might accidentally write one of these words in place of the other. It's also possible that back when you were learning to read and spell, you never truly distinguished between certain words.

If you didn't learn to distinguish one homophone from another during the years when your language skills were physically developing in your brain, it's okay. You can learn to make the distinction now. Our brains continue to develop!

Here's a list of homophones that are frequently confused for one another:

a lot, allot	hour, our	right, rite, write
ad, add	knew, new	scene, seen
all ready, already	know, no	stationary, stationery
brake, break	lead, led	their, there
buy, by	lessen, lesson	threw, through
cite, sight, site	male, mail	to, too, two
coarse, course	passed, past	wear, where
complement, compliment	peace, piece	weather, whether
do, due	plane, plain	wet, whet

forth, fourth	principal, principle	which, witch
hear, here	rain, reign, rein	whole, hole

Your Personal Homophone List

Now that you've been presented with this list, what should you do with it?

Get familiar with the words on the list. You don't have to memorize them. Just get to know them.

You can eliminate all the words you're sure of—sure of meaning, spelling, and usage. This will shorten your list.

Then grab something to write on and something to write with. Go ahead and make a new list of the words you're not sure of. It would be great if you could create your list the old-fashioned way, writing by hand. The physical process of writing out the words will help you incorporate their meanings. Later, you can type your list for extra reinforcement.

Next, we're going to talk about you and your dictionary… again.

Remember how I launched into a little dictionary lecture back in Chapter 1? At the risk of annoying you, I'm going to reinforce this: You'll find your dictionary to be an invaluable resource. Most dictionaries list each entry's part of speech right after its pronunciation. The part of speech is typically abbreviated and in italic type. Here's an example from thefreedictionary.com.[1]

(pees), *n.* **1.** freedom from war or hostilities.

---

1 For Abused, Confused, & Misused Words: *Abused, Confused, & Misused Words.* S.v. "peace." Retrieved September 9, 2021, from www.thefreedictionary.com/peace.

The "n." is an abbreviation for *noun*. A print dictionary will have a "how to use" section that explains its use of abbreviations. An online dictionary will likely have a "help" section that you can consult.

You can use your dictionary to look up the words from your personal homophone list.

You might like to write down their meanings, and their parts of speech. Many of the homophones are different parts of speech. For example, "by" is a preposition, and "buy" is a verb.

Aha! You're already a pro in this department. You recently completed a lesson on parts of speech!

Understanding a word's part of speech will help you know if you used the right homophone.

Beyond the homophones in the previous list, there are lots and lots more! You can add to your personal homophone list whenever you encounter a homophone you're unsure of, like *immanent/imminent* or *emigrate/immigrate*.

Going to your dictionary is active. We absorb things best when we're actively engaged in learning. Going to your dictionary is a form of active learning.

You might like to set a small challenge for yourself: While you're learning from this book, you could also learn one homophone a day.

In fact, even without trying to memorize, you'll find the simple process of looking over your personal list of homophones will help prepare you for any writing assignment that lies ahead, whether it's a term paper, a letter to your community board, a nurse's report, a teacher's note to parents, a blog article, or something else. The simple process of familiarizing yourself with the list will make you aware, and awareness gives you the power to check your writing.

That's grammar empowerment!

Lesson 2: Contractions vs. Possessive Pronouns

For now, it's important to distinguish between *contractions* and *possessive pronouns* that are homophones. In Chapter 3, we'll examine contractions and possessives from a different angle.

We'll look at your party invitation again to get a handle on the terms: "The honor of <u>you're</u> presence is requested at my dinner party."

In this draft, you've written *you're* (a contraction for *you are*) when you meant *your* (a possessive pronoun).

Contractions are made from two words that are put together. In putting them together, we omit a letter or two or three, and place an apostrophe where that letter or letters would have been. (If you're not sure what an apostrophe is, it's the punctuation mark that looks like a floating comma in the word *it's*.)

Contractions are shortcuts in everyday speaking and writing.

Example contractions:

> We change <u>they are</u> to <u>they're</u>. The apostrophe stands in place of the omitted letter *a*.

> We change <u>we are</u> to <u>we're</u>. The apostrophe stands in place of the omitted letter *a*.

> We change <u>I have</u> to <u>I've</u>. The apostrophe stands for two letters now, *h* and *a*.

> We change <u>I will</u> to <u>I'll</u>. The apostrophe stands for *w* and *i*.

Most contractions are probably familiar to you and don't give you any grammar trouble. Some contractions, however, sound just like other words. These contractions are homophones for a group of words called *possessive pronouns*.

What's a possessive pronoun? It's a word that indicates ownership, like *my, your, his, her,* and *our*. From the time we're toddlers and begin to use spoken language, we use possessives.

Example possessives:

> That's <u>my</u> block!

> We're in <u>your</u> house!

> Give him back <u>his</u> toys!

Here's where (not *wear*) we can get into trouble. Several possessive pronouns are homophones for words that are contractions. That's why we get confused and mix-ups occur.

Example contractions and possessives that are homophones:

> <u>They're</u> sounds just like <u>their</u>.

> <u>You're</u> sounds just like <u>your</u>.

It's easy to see how and why we confuse words like these. Maybe your hand has a mind of its own and begins writing the first few letters, and then it takes over based on sound rather than meaning or spelling. Once you become aware of these mix-ups, you can correct them. Step one is awareness. Step two is putting your awareness to work.

The following are frequently mixed-up pairs of contractions and possessives:

- it's, its
- they're, their
- you're, your
- who's, whose

This is a short list compared to the list of common homophones in Lesson 2. You can master this one quickly.

First, familiarize yourself with the list. Do you know which are the contractions and which are the possessives? Do you know how to use each one in a sentence?

Remember, to test if a contraction is right, you should be able to write it out and have a sensible sentence:

> <u>You're</u> going to the dinner party, right?

> <u>You are</u> going to the dinner party, right?

Second, eliminate the words you're sure of. Maybe you're already a master of contractions and possessive pronouns. Looking at this list may be enough to give you confidence that you know the difference and bolster you with a new ability to spot this type of mistake in your own writing. Sometimes we make mistakes even when we know better. That's okay! Now you can catch yourself in the act.

Third, if you're not yet confident, go ahead and make a list of the contraction/possessive pronoun pairs that confuse you. For reinforcement, write them out by hand.

Fourth, use your dictionary to look up each word remaining on your personal list. Your dictionary will tell you if it's a contraction or a possessive pronoun.

✍ Tip _____

The tiny words *its* and *it's* cause lots of trouble.

If you need help remembering which is which, keep these sentence examples in mind:

The spider wiggled <u>its</u> eight legs. (The legs belong to the spider.)

<u>It's</u> a scary spider! (You can replace *It's* with *It is*: It is a scary spider.)

Lesson 3: Other Confusables

Sometimes, a single letter or tiny sound separates one word from another. It's easy to understand why we so frequently interchange such words as *accept/except* or *conscience/conscious*. They're not pure homophones, but they're close.

If you mix up these words, you're not alone. Lots of people make the same mistakes. How often have you heard a well-spoken newscaster on TV or the radio say *lay* instead of *lie*?

Let's take another look at your invitation: "The honor of your presence is requested at my dinner party. RSVP to let me know that you are able to <u>except</u> my invitation."

In this version, you've asked your guests to omit your invitation. That's what *except* means in this context, but it's not what you wanted to say by requesting guests to RSVP. You really meant *accept*.

If we read aloud with an extra emphasis on distinct pronunciation, then we can hear the difference between words that sound very much alike. Give it a try with the word pairs in this next list:

a, an	diner, dinner	set, sit
accept, except	conscience, conscious	moral, morale

advice, advise	desert, dessert	personal, personnel
affect, effect	does, dose	quiet, quite
are, or, our	have, of	than, then
choose, chose	lay, lie	were, where
clothes, cloths	loose, lose	woman, women

If you can hear and/or see the difference, you're off to a great start. But if you can't hear or are otherwise unable to make a distinction, your dictionary (yeah, that again) can help with its pronunciation guide.

In addition to different pronunciations, most of the words in each pair represent different parts of speech. For example, in the *advice/advise* pair, *advice* is a noun and *advise* is a verb. Using the words in sentences helps us understand meaning and function:

> Your attorney offers good <u>advice</u> (noun).
>
> She <u>advises</u> (verb) you to explore your options.

Here's what you can do to master other confusables:

1. Make a list of the words you want to learn.
2. Look up each word in the dictionary, and find its meaning, pronunciation, and part of speech.
3. Set a learning challenge for yourself: Get familiar with a word a day.
4. Add to your personal list as you encounter more confusables when you're reading.

IN A NUTSHELL

In this chapter, we looked at three groups of commonly mixed-up words:

- homophones
- contractions vs. possessive pronouns
- other confusables

You learned that words can get mixed up because they sound alike or have very similar pronunciations and/or spellings. As listeners, we can't always distinguish differences in pronunciation and spelling. These differences are more obvious when we're writing or reading.

What can you do when presented with word choices, whether they're homophones, a pair of contractions and possessive pronouns, or other confusables? When you have word options and aren't confident, it's time for a date with your dictionary.

Most important, you've gained some awareness about the types of mistakes you might make. Awareness of these mix-ups allows you to take an extra look and spend an extra moment on your own writing. When you spot a word from your own list of mixed-up words, you can double-check that you've made the right choice.

Congratulations! You've gained the ability to determine which word is which (not *witch*).

Q: What's the real difference between *lie* and *lay*? Don't they mean the same thing?

A: *Lie* and *lay* are particularly confusing for several reasons. In addition to being mixed up with each other, both have more than one meaning.

Lie is a verb meaning "to lounge," but it's also a noun meaning "untruth." *Lay* is a verb meaning "to put or place," but it's also a verb meaning what a bird does when releasing an egg.

To further complicate things, *lay* is the past tense form of the verb *lie* when it means "to lounge." (We'll take a closer look at verb forms and tenses in future chapters.)

Most of our mix-ups occur with *lie* and *lay* when we incorrectly interchange the meaning of "lounge" with "put" or "place."

Lie is an intransitive verb. You can lounge in a certain way, such as luxuriously. You can lounge in a place, such as on the couch.

Lay is a transitive verb. Its meaning is not complete until it performs the action on something. You can put your car keys on the table. You can place your hands in your lap.

When you're tired, you *lie* down. But you *lay* your head down on the pillow. Still confused? When you're not sure which verb to use, try answering the old standby question: Do you mean lounge or put?

You can master this! Let's preserve the meanings of *lie* and *lay* for future generations!

Q: Can you explain when to use *affect* and when to use *effect*?

A: These confusables can be tricky.

Affect is a verb meaning "to have influence upon":

> The movie *affected* me tremendously: I couldn't stop crying all night.

Effect is a noun meaning result:

> The movie affected me tremendously. Its *effect* on me was my nonstop crying.

These are the two most common uses of *affect* and *effect*.

Additionally, *effect* is a verb, but it is used in a specialized way:

> The senator hoped to *effect* (bring about) a major societal change with her new bill.

When used as a verb, *effect* is almost always followed by "a change."

Affect as a verb also has another meaning and use:

> She *affects* an attitude of snobbery but, in fact, that's because she's quite shy.

Here, it means "feigns" or "puts on."

Affect is also a noun used in a specialized way, as a psychological term.

The affect/effect pair is a perfect example of why you sometimes need to dig into your dictionary. Not all definitions are straightforward, and some words are more than one part of speech. Don't worry: Most definitions are pretty clear.

If you understand the most common uses—*affect* as a verb meaning influence and *effect* as a noun meaning result—then you're 99 percent of the way home.

Q: I can't find *all ready* (two words) in my dictionary. How do I know whether to use it or *already* (one word)?

A: You may not find *all ready* (two words) in print dictionaries. These two words create a phrase we use this way:

> Are you *all ready* to go?

Depending on context, this could mean:

> Are you completely ready to go?

Or it could mean:

> Are all of you ready to go?

We use *already* (one word) this way:

> I *already* ate lunch.

This means:

> I ate lunch (completed the action) before now.

If a regular dictionary fails you, try a dictionary of idioms. You can find this for free online.

Q: Why doesn't the possessive *its* have an apostrophe?

A: In English, we have a group of words called *possessive pronouns*. The concept of "possession" is built into their meaning, so we don't do double-duty by adding an apostrophe.

Just as possessive pronouns *his* and *hers* don't have an apostrophe, gender-neutral *its* doesn't either.

Q: How do I know when to use *every day* or *everyday*?

A: This question relates to homophones and to parts of speech. To answer it, we need to do two things: 1) look at the words in context; and 2) understand their parts of speech.

> Will you be going to tourist attractions every day when you're on vacation?

In this example, two words are right: adverb *every* plus noun *day*. Try a substitution strategy: You could substitute the adverb *daily* and have a sensible sentence.

> When you go on vacation, you'll want a few <u>everyday</u> things with you, like a pack of tissues.

In this example, one word is right: adjective *everyday*. Try a substitution strategy: You could substitute the adjective *common* and have a sensible sentence.

If you're not sure which is right, your dictionary will come to your rescue!

Chapter 2 Quiz

Question 1

Choose the correct word:

"You imagined receiving many (complements/compliments) on the cake you baked."

    a. complements

    b. compliments

Question 2

Choose the correct word:

"You rented a party tent so that you wouldn't have to cancel (dew/do/due) to bad weather."

    a. dew

    b. do

    c. due

Question 3

Choose the correct word:

"Maybe you should (of/have) thrown a party that wasn't quite so fancy."

    a. of

    b. have

Answer Key: Q1:b Q2:c Q3:b

IT'S OR ITS?

(contractions and possessives)

Introduction

> **KEYWORDS:**
>
> ◊ homophone ◊ possessive pronoun
>
> ◊ contraction

In the last chapter, we briefly discussed the apostrophe when we looked at homophone pairs like its/it's and your/you're. Now it's time to learn more about this little punctuation mark.

(Reminder: The apostrophe is the mark that looks like a floating comma in the word *it's*.)

Aunt Felicity has come for a visit and is going to kick off our grammar lesson. She has insomnia and asks you to join her for a meal in the middle of the night. The two of you decide to go to an all-night diner.

Aunt Felicity has a big appetite and orders a substantial meal. It's a combo served in a bowl: a tofu, vegetable, and brown rice stir-fry piled on a bed of mixed greens. (Aunt Felicity's a healthy eater.)

You didn't know you were hungry, but this sounds good to you. So you order a combo bowl too, though you want white rice instead of brown.

You and Aunt Felicity have a chance to talk while waiting for your orders to arrive.

"You're doing well at your new job?" she asks.

"Yes, I'm doing great!"

"That's wonderful," Aunt Felicity says.

You might be familiar with contractions like *you're* and *I'm* and *that's*.

A contraction results when we combine two separate words to create one and use the apostrophe to stand in for the omitted letter or letters:

- you're = you are
- I'm = I am
- that's = that is

Contractions speed up our speech and give it a natural, informal tone.

After about fifteen minutes, the server comes back to your table with your meals.

He wants to know who ordered the combo bowl with brown rice.

"That's my aunt's order," you say to the server.

"The one with white rice is my nephew's," Aunt Felicity tells him.

The words *aunt's* and *nephew's* are possessives.

It's important to keep our possessives straight so that we're sure whose order is whose. People often want to make clear that something belongs to them and not to somebody else.

About now, you might be wondering why contractions and possessives were brought together in this chapter. It's because they have something in common: Both are created with the apostrophe.

In this chapter, you'll learn how and when to make contractions, and you'll also learn how to make possessives. Let's get started!

Lesson 1: Common Contractions

When we merge two words to make a new one, and insert an apostrophe to represent the omitted letter or letters, we have a contraction. *He'll* and *shouldn't* and *where's* are examples.

To get more familiar with this concept, let's look at three groups of common contractions.

In this first group, each contraction begins with a pronoun. We'll call this group *pronoun contractions*:

he	• he'd (he had or he would) • he'll (he will) • he's (he has or he is)
I	• I'd (I had or I would) • I'll (I will) • I'm (I am) • I've (I have)
it	• it'll (it will) • it's (it has or it is)
she	• she'd (she had or she would) • she'll (she will) • she's (she has or she is)
they	• they'd (they had or they would) • they'll (they will) • they're (they are) • they've (they have)
we	• we'd (we had or we would) • we'll (we will) • we're (we are) • we've (we have)

who	• who'd (who had or who would) • who's (who has or who is)
you	• you'd (you would) • you'll (you will) • you're (you are) • you've (you have)

In parentheses to the right of each contraction, you'll find the two words from which the contraction is made. This should help you be aware of which letter or letters the apostrophe represents. For example, when you look at *we'd*, the apostrophe stands in for the omitted letters *woul* in *would*.

When you make a contraction, the placement of the apostrophe is fixed. If you misplace the apostrophe, the result is a spelling mistake:

> incorrect: w'ed
>
> correct: we'd

In our second group, each contraction comes from merging a verb and the word *not*. We'll call this group *negative contractions*:

- **aren't (are not)**
- **can't (cannot)**
- **couldn't (could not)**
- **didn't (did not)**
- **don't (do not)**
- **hadn't (had not)**
- **haven't (have not)**
- **shouldn't (should not)**
- **won't (will not)**
- **wouldn't (would not)**

(Note that we have an outlier with *won't*. The spelling change that takes place when turning *will not* into a contraction is the result of the linguistic journey it took from Old English.)

Next we have contractions made with *here*, *there*, or *where* plus verb *is*:

- here's (here is)
- there's (there is)
- where's (where is)

And we have one that stands alone:

- let's (let us)

 Tip _____

1. Contractions require the apostrophe.
2. It's important to put the apostrophe where it belongs; a misplaced apostrophe equals a spelling mistake.
3. Verb *lets* is different from contraction *let's*.

    lets = verb

    let's = verb *let* + pronoun *us*

Formal vs. Informal Writing

Now let's talk about when to use contractions and when not to use them.

When you consider whether or not to use contractions, you'll want to think about the purpose of your writing and the audience for your words. Are you talking to a friend on the phone, writing a casual letter to a family member, or chatting with office mates during a coffee break? An informal style using contractions would be A-OK.

Contractions are language shortcuts. It's comfortable and acceptable to use them in writing and speaking most of the time. We use contractions in our informal, everyday communications; however, we typically don't use them in formal writing such as a term paper, a business report, or a letter of complaint to a local congressperson. For any of those writing jobs, convention calls for a more formal tone.

Let's examine the following short paragraph in two forms, without contractions and with contractions.

Without contractions:

> You are going to get breakfast right away. You are absolutely ravenous this morning. You hope your favorite fast-food place will not have a huge waiting line by the time you get there. You will have to wait for a very, very long time if it does. You have had to wait for a long time in the past when you did not get there before rush hour.

With contractions:

> You're going to get breakfast right away. You're absolutely ravenous this morning. You hope your favorite fast-food place won't have a huge waiting line by the time you get there. You'll have to wait for a very, very long time if it does. You've had to wait for a long time in the past when you didn't get there before rush hour.

The first paragraph reads as stilted, choppy, and somewhat formal. We'd probably opt for the second paragraph. It reflects someone's natural way of speaking.

As a writer, you set the level of formality you want to achieve. Reading your work aloud is one of the best ways to determine if your writing meets your goal. You can read it to yourself or to a willing listener.

The bottom line: Contractions are appropriate most of the time. In a few formal writing environments, we don't use them. Now that you have contractions under your belt, you're ready for possessives!

Lesson 2: Regular Possessives

The small apostrophe has a big job. We use it to create contractions, and we use it to create *possessives*.

What's a possessive? In grammar, a possessive is a word that indicates ownership. Sometimes this ownership is clear-cut: *actor's* lines, *brother's* friend, or *supervisor's* orders. Sometimes the concept of ownership is more abstract: one *day's* work, four *weeks'* pay, or *journey's* end. We use a little imagination for those.

In this lesson, we'll take a look at where to place the apostrophe to make singular and plural possessives, like *girl's* and *girls'* or *family's* and *families'*.

(In a later chapter, we'll look at *possessive pronouns*, which already have the idea of possession built into their meaning and don't use an apostrophe. Examples are the possessive pronouns *his*, *hers*, and *yours*.)

Singular Possessives

Singular means *one*. We're going to look at how to make one person or thing into a possessive.

The rule is simple. Add *'s* (apostrophe plus the letter *s*).

The word *friend* becomes *friend's* when you want to write, "I'm using my <u>friend's</u> recipe to make mashed turnips."

Note that the idea of singular applies to the possessive, not to the number of things he, she, they, or it possess(es):

- <u>person's</u> mood
- <u>person's</u> moods

A singular possessive can own one thing (mood) or more than one thing (moods).

The rule for making singular possessives is easy to latch onto. Just remember this: When you want to show that something or someone owns something else, add *'s* (apostrophe plus the letter *s*).

Plurals

While *singular* means *one*, *plural* means *more than one*. In English, we have a fairly simple spelling convention for making plurals. Add the letter *s* to a word to transform it from a singular to a plural: one *carrot*, three *carrots*.

This simple spelling convention takes care of the majority of words, but not all. Sometimes we have to add more than the letter *s*. We have to add *es*: one *potato*, two *potato<u>es</u>*; or one *pinch* of salt, two *pinch<u>es</u>* of salt. And sometimes we have to eliminate a *y* ending and add *ies* for the plural: one *candy*, three *cand<u>ies</u>*.

These plural words are examples of variations in our spelling conventions. But they all end in *s*. We call these words *regular plurals*.

(Some plural words don't have an *s* ending. Examples are *men*, *women*, and *children*. We'll cover these *irregular plurals* in the next lesson.)

Make abbreviations plural the same way you make
other nouns plural, by adding *s*: one *FAQ*, eight *FAQs*;
one *PhD*, two *PhDs*.

Plural or Possessive?

It's easy to confuse plurals and possessives. After all, most
plurals end in *s*, as do most possessives.

To determine if a word is a possessive or a plural, we look at
it in context to figure out its role. Does someone or something
own something? If the answer is yes, then it's a possessive and
needs an apostrophe. If the answer is no, then it's probably a
plural and shouldn't have an apostrophe.

Take a look at the following sentence and focus on
the words *cooks* and *instructor's* to distinguish between
possessives and plurals:

> All <u>cooks</u> who plan on attending the <u>instructor's</u>
> seminar next week, please fill out an
> application form.

The word *cooks* is simply a plural, but *instructor's* is a
possessive. The seminar belongs to the instructor—the
instructor owns the seminar.

If you've been using an apostrophe to make a word into a
plural, then today's the day you're going to quit.

No to this:

> You've invited <u>friend's</u> and <u>family member's</u> over
> to watch a movie.

Yes to this:

> You've invited <u>friends</u> and <u>family members</u> over
> to watch a movie.

Plural Possessives

Since you've been refreshed on forming regular singular
possessives and on making a singular word into a plural by
adding *s* or *es* or converting a *y* to *ies*, now you're ready for
plural possessives.

The basic rule is simple: First make the word plural, and
then add the apostrophe. Let's do it with the word chef:

- singular=chef
- plural=chefs
- singular possessive=chef's
- plural possessive=chefs'

Now let's do it with a word that ends in y, family:

- singular=family
- plural=families
- singular possessive=family's
- plural possessive=families'

(There's only one Aunt Felicity, so we won't turn her into
a plural.)

When we create a plural possessive, the idea of plural
applies to the possessive, like *chefs'* and *families'*, not to the
number of things owned. A plural possessive may own one or
more things:

- <u>chefs'</u> kitchen (one thing)
- <u>chefs'</u> tools (more than one)
- <u>families'</u> mailbox (one thing)
- <u>families'</u> bicycles (more than one)

We've reviewed the basic rules for forming possessives. Here are the most important basics:

> To make a singular possessive, add apostrophe *s*.

> To make a plural possessive, first make the word plural, and then add an apostrophe.

These two rules govern regular possessives and equip you with about 90 percent of what you need to know to make possessives. You're already on your way to being a possessives pro!

Next, we'll look at irregular and unusual possessives.

Lesson 3: Irregular and Unusual Possessives

Whew! Just when you thought you knew everything you needed to know about the apostrophe and forming possessives, well, yes, there's more! English is a language with lots of irregularities.

You've learned how to form regular singular and plural possessives. Now we'll review the conventions for other types of possessives. We'll look at the following situations to see how to turn them into possessives:

- singular words that end in the letter *s*
- plurals with endings other than the letter *s*

- proper nouns
- compound nouns

Don't worry. The list isn't endless. You can shoot for a comfort level with this material; you don't need to memorize it. A reasonable goal is to recognize irregular or uncommon possessives and know it's time to consult a resource if your memory banks are overflowing.

I'll tell you up front that various stylebooks and grammar guides will present variations for almost any rule you meet in this lesson.

Here you'll learn the basic rules, with the understanding that there are often different approaches.

Singular Words Ending in *s*

How do you make such a word into a possessive? Add *'s*, just as you do when you make a regular singular into a possessive:

- boss → boss's
- class → class's
- bus → bus's

Okay, the truth is some style guides tell us not to use *'s* with words that end in double *s*, like *boss*, and instead direct us to use the apostrophe only. I choose to stick with the classic *'s* for the sake of sound and consistency. Whatever style you follow, consistency is key.

Plurals That Don't End in *s*

Some plural words have an ending other than *s*. How do you make a word like that into a possessive? Add *'s*:

- children → children's
- people → people's
- alumni → alumni's

Proper Nouns

You might remember proper nouns. We discussed them in Chapter 1 when we reviewed parts of speech. As distinguished from a common noun, a proper noun is a particular person, place, or thing that's capitalized: *President Lincoln*, *South Dakota*, or the movie title *The Lord of the Rings*.

It's easy to make a proper noun into a possessive. We treat proper nouns the same way we treat common nouns.

Add *'s* to a singular proper noun:

- Newton → Newton's
- California → California's
- Parthenon → Parthenon's

To make a proper noun into a plural possessive, first make sure to add the plural ending, and then add the apostrophe:

- Young → Youngs → Youngs'
- Garcia → Garcias → Garcias'
- Jones → Joneses → Joneses'
- Calloway → Calloways → Calloways'

Add the letters *es* to make the plural of a singular name that ends with *ch, s, sh, ss, x,* or *z*: one *Katz*, two *Katzes*.

Keep the *y* and add *s* to make the plural of a singular name that ends in *y*: one *Colby*, two *Colbys*.

Compound Nouns

When we use a conjunction to join two or more nouns, the result is a *compound noun*.

If ownership is joint, add *'s* to the last noun. Let's assume Ed and Stanley are equal partners in that diner where Aunt Felicity enjoyed her meal in the middle of the night:

> Ed and Stanley's diner.

If you want to make clear, however, that each has his own diner or his own pair of shoes, then add *'s* for each noun:

> Ed's and Stanley's diners. (Each owns a diner.)

> Ed's and Stanley's shoes. (Each has a pair of shoes.)

IN A NUTSHELL

We've covered lots of uses of the apostrophe.

In this chapter, you learned how to make contractions. Contractions are simple language shortcuts.

You also learned how to form possessives, which are words that indicate ownership. Like contractions, most possessives are formed with the apostrophe.

One group of possessives—possessive pronouns—don't use the apostrophe because the idea of ownership is already built into their meaning.

We also looked at some simple but common misuses of the apostrophe. In contractions, it's important to put the apostrophe in the right place. If we don't, we create a spelling error. Sometimes, we confuse a simple plural for a possessive or confuse a singular possessive for a plural.

Even when we're comfortable with contractions and possessives, it's easy to make a mistake. If you catch yourself misplacing the apostrophe, you may be tired, rushed, or distracted. That's why it's good to check your writing, even if it's casual, such as an email to a friend.

By working through this chapter, you've developed the ability to check your own work for the grammatical use of contractions and possessives. It's great to be able to see your mistakes… and to know how to fix them. Reading your work aloud can help you detect mistakes that are easily overlooked during a silent reading.

You've learned that consistency is important when style guides differ on the rules.

Who knew there was so much to learn about such a little punctuation mark? Now that you know all about the apostrophe and its proper place in contractions and possessives, you're ready for subjects and predicates in our next chapter.

Now's a good time to mention pacing. There's a lot to learn in every chapter. If you're working through an entire chapter in one sitting and find yourself overwhelmed, try working in shorter sessions. Two or three lessons in one sitting may be just right for you. Then you can come back for more.

I know you're excited to get to the next grammar topic, but I encourage you to take your time.

FAQs

Q: What about double contractions like shouldn't've?

A: They're considered very informal, so it's best not to use them when you want to show off your writing skills. You can have fun using them in casual writing and in dialogue.

Q: Why doesn't *will not* become *won't*? Doesn't that break spelling rules for making a contraction?

A: Some of our spelling conventions in English have their roots in very old forms of the language, and that's what accounts for the odd spelling.

Q: How do I make a number or a letter into a plural?

A: Numbers are easy! Add *s*: 5s, 15s, and 20s. Letters are a little more complicated, and style guides differ on how to handle them. Generally, add *'s* to make a lowercase letter plural: x's, y's, and z's. The apostrophe helps us avoid a misreading, especially with *a*'s and *i*'s. To make an uppercase letter plural, you can skip the apostrophe or use it. But if you skip it, watch out for *As* or *Is* that start a sentence. Whichever style you choose, consistency is key.

Chapter 3 Quiz

Question 1

Read the sentence and then choose the correct possessive:

"Celeste has a hover board, and Hakim has a hover board."

    a. Celeste's and Hakim's hover boards

    b. Celeste and Hakim's hover boards

Question 2

"Coworker's suggestions" is an example of which of the following?

    a. simple plural

    b. singular possessive

    c. plural possessive

Question 3

Which contraction has a misplaced apostrophe?

    a. they've

    b. shouldn't

    c. did'nt

Answer Key: Q1:a Q2:b Q3:c

CHAPTER 4

TEAM WORK

(subjects and
predicates)

Introduction

KEYWORDS:

◊ subject

◊ predicate

◊ sentence structure

◊ compound subject

◊ compound predicate

◊ verb phrase

◊ object of a preposition

◊ prepositional phrase

◊ invisible subject

◊ imperative

In this chapter, you're going to discover *subjects* and *predicates*. They're the foundation of sentence structure.

Understanding sentence structure without knowing the basics is a lot like trying to navigate a brand-new, gigantic superstore. If you're making a quick run to that store to pick up some staples like cereal and juice, it's important to know where to find them. Otherwise, you could spend hours weaving in and out of aisles without ever locating what you came for.

Likewise, subjects and predicates are the staples of sentence structure. The rest of a sentence is built on them.

Why should you be able to recognize subjects and predicates? They're the two ingredients required to make a sentence complete. They work together as a team.

We need to understand team subject-predicate to be sure we're writing complete sentences and to be sure we're using good grammar to end or connect complete thoughts.

Our work here sets the stage for upcoming chapters. Just about everything else we'll look at in this book will have some relationship to subjects and predicates.

You may have noticed that each chapter is divided into several short lessons. I encourage you to take your time and take a break often. There's a lot to learn. Slow and steady is the way to go.

Ready? Let's find out what subjects and predicates are!

Lesson 1: Getting to Know Subjects and Predicates

Every grammatical sentence has two parts: *subject* and *predicate*:

> The predicate tells us what's happening.

> The subject tells us who or what makes it happen.

You can think of the subject as the actor and the predicate as the action. Here's a simple sentence to demonstrate:

> Mr. Gray **teaches.**

> > subject = Mr. Gray

> > predicate = teaches

Teaches is the action that's happening. *Mr. Gray* is the actor who makes it happen.

We have a complete, simple sentence.

Let's look at a busier one:

> Your old high school English teacher Mr. Gray **nowadays teaches English at a school for young language learners in Dubai.**

The beginning phrase "Your old high school English teacher Mr. Gray" is all about Mr. Gray and makes the *complete subject*. The rest of the sentence is about what Mr. Gray is doing and makes the *complete predicate*.

We're going to focus on the *simple subject* (Mr. Gray) and the *simple predicate* (teaches). And I'll keep it simple and call them *subject* and *predicate*.

You may recall from your review of parts of speech in Chapter 1 that *Mr. Gray* is a noun (a proper noun) and *teaches* is a verb.

And you may recall that a noun and a verb can make a complete sentence. So why are we talking about subjects and predicates instead of nouns and verbs?

Here's why:

1. When we look at a sentence, we might see any number of nouns. Maybe one of them is the subject. But it's very possible something else is the subject.

   Not all subjects are nouns, and not all nouns are subjects.

2. Likewise, a sentence could have any number of verbs, but some of them might not be the predicate.

   Predicates are always verbs, but not all verbs are predicates.

I hope that's not making your head spin.

It's the same kind of logic we can use back in the kitchen:

1 Not all chefs are bakers, and not all bakers are chefs.

2. Broccoli is always a vegetable, but not all vegetables are broccoli.

Food and grammar have a lot in common!

Lesson 2: Predicate Basics: Action Verbs and Linking Verbs

In English, our sentences are usually structured this way: subject-predicate. We read from left to right, so we generally encounter a subject first and a predicate second.

However, you might find it easier to locate the predicate first and the subject second. Once you find what's happening (predicate), you can find who or what makes it happen (subject).

This strategy isn't set in stone. Doing things the other way around is just fine. You can experiment to learn what works best for you.

Let's try finding the predicate first. How do you do that? You start by looking for what's happening in the sentence, and you zoom in on the verb or verbs.

You guessed it! Your parts-of-speech knowledge from Chapter 1 is going to come in handy now. And I'll remind you of a little something: It's okay if you don't automatically remember everything we covered about parts of speech. If you need to refer to Chapter 1 to refresh your memory, that's just fine. This is a grammar refresher! You're not expected to have a brain like a computer.

Some people have super memories. They read something once and remember it forever. But the truth is most of us need to acquaint ourselves with information, and reacquaint ourselves, and maybe even do it again before that information begins to stick.

You've learned that verbs are words that show action or work as links. Let's look at a few sentences to ensure you understand action verbs and linking verbs and recognize when they're working as predicates.

And to do that, let's use the familiar terrain of the kitchen again:

> You <u>stir</u> the spaghetti in the pot. (*Stir* is an action verb.)
>
> The water <u>boils</u>. (*Boils* is an action verb.)
>
> The pasta <u>smells</u> good. (*Smells* is a linking verb.)
>
> I <u>am</u> ready for dinner. (*Am* is a linking verb.)

Many linking verbs are based on the verb *be*. Examples are *is*, *am*, *are*, and *was*. They're fairly easy to spot. But how do you recognize other linking verbs?

In almost all sentences with other single-word linking verbs, you can substitute the words is/are or equal/equals, and the sentence will still make grammatical sense.

> The pasta <u>smells</u> good. = The pasta <u>is</u> good.
>
> Aunt Felicity <u>seems</u> like a nice person. = Aunt Felicity <u>equals</u> a nice person.

In a way, linking verbs equate the subject to what's on the other side of the link:

> Wow, that pasta <u>tastes</u> good!
>
> pasta = good

We're reinforcing your knowledge of linking verbs because, as you begin to look at sentence structure and pick out predicates, you want to be able to spot linking verbs right along with action verbs.

You're sailing down the predicate aisle!

Lesson 3: More About Predicates

So far, we've looked at predicates that are only one word. Now let's look at predicates that are more than one word: *compound predicates* and *verb phrases*.

Compound Predicates

Often, a sentence has more than one predicate.

When we join two predicates, the result is a *compound predicate*:

> Good cooks <u>grow and use</u> fresh herbs.
> (The predicates are *grow* and *use*.)

> Who <u>scrubs and rinses</u> the dishes?
> (The predicates are *scrubs* and *rinses*.)

Notice how conjunction *and* joins the predicates? (Your knowledge of parts of speech is coming in handy again. You know that conjunctions are words that join.)

Conjunctions can join predicates to create a compound predicate!

> predicate and predicate = compound predicate

Verb Phrases

A predicate can be more than one word.

We can call a multi-word predicate a *verb phrase*.

Here's an example:

Tonight you <u>will read</u> an enjoyable magazine.

In this sentence, the predicate is *will read*.

Perhaps you're tired of the superstore and cooks and the kitchen and are feeling sleepy now. Let's take the verb *sleep* to generate more examples of verb phrases:

I <u>am sleeping</u>.

She <u>has slept</u>.

He <u>will sleep</u>.

The children <u>should have slept</u>.

In each sentence example, the verb phrase is the predicate.

It's time to find out who or what brings the predicates to life! (If you're thinking *subjects*, you're on target.)

Lesson 4: Subject Basics: Nouns and Pronouns

You know that a subject makes its predicate happen, whether the predicate is an action verb or a linking verb. A noun can be a subject, and a pronoun can be a subject.

Example noun subject:

The <u>children</u> eat dinner early, at 5:30 p.m. (The subject is *children*, a noun.)

Example pronoun subject:

> *You* eat later, at 7:00 p.m. (The subject is *you*, a pronoun.)

Just as we can join predicates to make a compound predicate, we can join subjects to create a *compound subject*.

Example compound subject:

> The <u>children and you</u> like to eat together. (The subjects are *children* and *you*.)

> subject and subject = compound subject

Invisible Subjects

You already know that a complete sentence requires a subject and a predicate.

Some complete sentences look like they're breaking the rule. Sentences that issue commands often leave out the subject:

> Get to the dinner table immediately!

> Please begin eating.

In these sentences, the subject is implied. We understand that the subject is the pronoun *you*:

> <u>You</u> get to the dinner table immediately!

> <u>You</u> please begin eating.

Here's another command:

> Put your toys away before bed!

This means:

> <u>You</u> put your toys away before bed!

We call a command sentence an *imperative*. It's good to be aware if you encounter an imperative that the subject might be implied rather than written.

Implied subjects are invisible.

Lesson 5: Tricky Subjects and Predicates

In this lesson, we'll look at some tricky subjects and predicates. Don't worry, though. You're up to the challenge. Once you know how to find them, they'll seem less tricky.

Remember, when you look at a sentence, you may find it makes sense to locate the predicate first and then figure out who or what is making it happen (the subject).

Reverse Order: Predicate Before Subject

What happens when our sentences deviate from the standard subject-predicate order? Sentences can work in "reverse order" and still be grammatical. These sentences may be statements or questions, and they usually start with one of these cue words: where, there, here, or how.

> Where are my scissors?

> There's the missing fork!

At first glance, you may think that the words *Where* and *There* are the respective subjects of their sentences because they precede the predicate. To find the subject in a sentence like these, try changing the word order. Sometimes you can flip the sentence, but you might have to play around a little with the word order:

> Where is my eyeglass case? → My <u>eyeglass case</u> is where?
>
> Here it is! → <u>It</u> is here!

Now we can clearly see that the words *eyeglass case* and *it* are subjects.

Object of a Preposition

During your review of parts of speech, you learned about prepositions. Prepositions almost never stand alone. Prepositions are a way of placing one thing in relation to another, and the something that follows a preposition is called the *object of a preposition*. The whole package is a prepositional phrase:

- on the stove
- in the oven
- under the fridge

The rules of grammar say that a sentence subject can't be in a prepositional phrase. When a prepositional phrase comes right before a predicate, we have to look carefully to find the true subject.

> Here's an example:

> Many <u>of my successes</u> began as experiments.

At first glance, the word *successes* may appear to be the subject of the sentence. It's right next to the verb, making it look like the subject. But you know that a subject can't be in a prepositional phrase, and the prepositional phrase is "of my successes."

How do you find a subject in a sentence like this? By eliminating the prepositional phrase. Then it's easy to find the subject:

> Many ~~of my successes~~ began as experiments.
>
> <u>Many</u> began as experiments.

Here's another example:

> The casserole ~~in the microwave~~ will be ready soon.

The <u>casserole</u> will be ready soon.

This simple strategy will help you find the true sentence subject and not be fooled by a prepositional phrase. It's going to help you down the track, when we talk about subject-verb agreement.

IN A NUTSHELL

You learned how to locate the basic parts of sentence structure, subjects and predicates. You now have a grammar advantage.

You can find the predicate by answering: "What's happening?"

You can find the subject by answering: "Who or what makes it happen?"

You've been introduced to simple subjects and predicates, compound subjects and predicates, and predicates that are verb phrases. You've also learned how to handle some tricky situations.

Sentences can be very long and complicated. In this chapter, we looked at short, relatively simple sentences. They're a starting point.

A reminder: The terminology in the course is simply a way for us to talk about words in a sentence. As you go on to the next chapter, try not to worry if the lexicon isn't always on the tip of your tongue. Aim for familiarity as you learn more about grammar. You're here to learn, not to memorize. You can always return to a chapter whenever you need to.

FAQs

Q: I've heard the terms *finite* and *nonfinite* verbs. What are they, and can they be predicates?

A: A *finite verb* can be a linking verb or an action verb, and it can be a sentence predicate. We looked at finite verbs in this chapter. A *nonfinite verb* is another name for a *verbal*. It's a verb form, but it's not working as a verb, and it can't be a predicate.

Q: What's the difference between a linking verb and a helping verb?

A: A linking verb can function solo as the main verb in a sentence. A helping verb (a.k.a. an *auxiliary verb*) works with a main verb, and together they create a verb phrase, as in these examples:

- **will be** arriving
- **do** hope
- **was** seen

Chapter 4 Quiz

Question 1

Find the subject:

"You are you and always will be!"

    a. You

    b. are

    c. you

Question 2

Find the predicate:

"Experienced cooks prefer fresh herbs."

    a. Experienced

    b. cooks

    c. prefer

Question 3

A predicate can be which of the following?

    a. action verb only

    b. action or linking verb

    c. linking verb only

Answer Key: Q1:a Q2:c Q3:b

CHAPTER 5

AS YOU WERE SAYING

(sentence fragments)

Introduction

KEYWORDS:

◊ sentence fragment

◊ complete sentence

◊ phrase

◊ clause

◊ subordinating conjunction

◊ relative pronoun

A freshly baked cherry pie sits in the middle of the table. The pie has been out of the oven for an hour, and it's just the right temperature.

You can see the pie. You can smell the pie. You're ready for a slice. The crust and the filling complement each other perfectly. These two parts of the pie make the pie whole.

The picture is complete.

Aunt Felicity slices and serves the pie. (Yup, she's back for yet another visit!) As she hands you a plate, you look down and experience a great sense of disappointment. Your plate holds a single cherry. Not a slice. Not even some cherry filling on a small, broken piece of crust. Just a cherry. (Aunt Felicity is great at baking but not at dishing out pie. She got distracted by a butterfly outside the kitchen window.)

This single cherry is not a serving of pie! It's not the slice you were anticipating.

If we liken a slice of pie to a sentence, then we can also liken that lone cherry on your plate to a *sentence fragment*. Crust and filling together make a complete slice; subject and predicate make a complete sentence. If either is missing, you have a sentence fragment.

Sentence fragments are missing something.

If you write sentence fragments, you have a lot of company. In most writing, fragments are ungrammatical. In many cases, fragments also don't make sense and leave readers with some unanswered questions.

Occasionally, fragments are acceptable, and we'll take a look at when and where.

In this chapter, you'll learn:

- how to spot sentence fragments
- how to turn them into complete sentences

Here's some good news: As of Chapter 4, you're practically an expert at recognizing subjects and predicates. Because you know that together they make a sentence complete, you're already equipped to spot a sentence that's incomplete, a.k.a. a sentence fragment.

Lesson 1: The Case of the Missing Predicate

You know that a complete sentence requires a subject and a predicate. In this lesson, we'll take a look at fragments that are missing a predicate.

Let's use three examples from the introduction to this chapter:

1. Not a slice.
2. Not even some cherry filling on a small, broken piece of crust.
3. Just a cherry.

Each of these fragments is nothing more than a *phrase*.

What's a phrase? A phrase is a group of related words. Those words aren't a complete sentence because they don't include both a subject and a predicate.

Examples 1 and 3 are easy to recognize as phrases.

A long phrase like example 2 might be a little harder to recognize as a fragment. Long phrases can masquerade as complete sentences. But you're not going to let length fool you. A phrase isn't a complete sentence, no matter how many words it includes.

Each of these phrases could be the subject of a sentence and simply needs the addition of a predicate to morph into a complete sentence!

The Solution

How do we correct a fragment that's missing its predicate? One way is simple: Add a predicate.

Let's transform the fragments by giving each a predicate:

1. Not a slice. → Not a slice <u>graced</u> my plate.
2. Not even some cherry filling on a small, broken piece of crust. → Not even some cherry filling on a small, broken piece of crust <u>waited</u> for my fork.
3. Just a cherry. → Just a cherry <u>stared</u> up at me.

Problem solved! The sentences are now complete; each has a subject *and* a predicate.

Context

There are other ways to correct these fragments, and to use those methods, we need to examine the fragments in context. We look at what comes before and after them. Then we can sensibly incorporate the fragments and make whole sentences.

So let's look at our sample fragments in relation to the full sentence that precedes them:

> Your plate holds a single cherry. *Not a slice. Not even some cherry filling on a small, broken piece of crust. Just a cherry.*

Here are two possible solutions:

> Your plate holds a single cherry—not a slice, not even a bit of filling adhering to a broken piece of crust—just a cherry.

In this first example, we've inserted the fragments into a complete sentence by using a dash on either side. (We'll talk about the dash in upcoming chapters.)

> Your plate holds a single cherry. Not a slice, not even a bit of filling adhering to a broken piece of crust, just a cherry <u>sits on</u> your plate.

In this second example, we've attached the first two fragments to the third, and we've added a predicate (and a preposition).

These examples present two solutions, not all solutions. Almost always, there are alternative ways to rewrite sentences. A little imagination plus a little grammar can add up to a variety of good, new sentences.

Eliminating sentence fragments achieves more than making complete sentences. It gives you the opportunity to use some interesting and active verbs in your writing.

Lesson 2: The Case of the Missing Subject

The give-and-take of conversation makes fragments natural when we're speaking. But what's natural in speaking can be weird or confusing in writing.

A sentence fragment could be missing a subject. This type of fragment tends to be easier to spot than a fragment missing a predicate.

A fragment without a subject could be the answer to a question:

> What do hikers do for recreation?
>
> > Hike in the woods.
>
> Could you follow up on some phone calls?
>
> > Yes, will do it as soon as possible.

A fragment without a subject could be an incomplete continuation of a preceding sentence:

> She was in the kitchen staring at both pies.
>
> > Needed to cool for an hour.
>
> The cat began meowing as soon as the car pulled into the driveway.
>
> > Then excitedly ran in circles when the key turned in the lock.

The Solution

We can easily correct this kind of fragment by adding a subject.

> Hike in the woods. → <u>Hikers</u> hike in the woods.
>
> Yes, will do it as soon as possible. → Yes, <u>I</u> will do it as soon as possible.
>
> Needed to cool for an hour. → <u>They</u> needed to cool for an hour.
>
> Then excitedly ran in circles when the key turned in the lock. → Then the <u>cat</u> excitedly ran in circles when the key turned in the lock.

These examples are only suggestions. There's almost always more than one way to turn a fragment into a complete sentence.

Lesson 3: Understanding Clauses

We've looked at fragments that are missing a subject or predicate. Next we'll look at fragments that include a subject and a predicate but still don't measure up to a complete sentence.

These fragments are a little trickier to recognize, but we're going to pinpoint some words that provide clues.

Once you can spot these clues, you'll be a pro at recognizing fragments that try to pass themselves off as complete sentences.

But first, it's time to add to our grammar lexicon and meet the *clause*.

Independent Clause vs. Dependent Clause

What's a clause?

Like a phrase, a clause is a group of words working together. But unlike a phrase, a clause contains a subject *and* a predicate.

A clause that can stand alone as a complete sentence is called an *independent clause*:

> You are a grammar student. = independent clause

A clause that begins with a word or phrase that makes it dependent on another clause is called a *dependent clause*:

> Because you are a grammar student. =
> dependent clause

Don't be fooled by a capital letter at the start and a period at the end.

Let's reinforce important points about clauses:

> An independent clause can stand on its own as a complete sentence.
>
> A dependent clause can't stand on its own as a complete sentence.

And let's add an important piece of information:

> A dependent clause standing by itself is a sentence fragment.

✍ Tip

> Many grammar guides use the term *subordinate clause* instead of dependent clause. These are two names for the same thing.

Understanding dependent clauses versus independent clauses will not only help you fix sentence fragments but also help prepare you for the next chapter, where we work on correcting run-on sentences.

Let's reveal some clues so you can recognize dependent clauses.

Lesson 4: Fragment Clues: Subordinating Conjunctions

First we'll look at fragments that begin with a *subordinating conjunction*.

You're familiar with coordinating conjunctions like the words *and*, *but*, and *for*. These conjunctions join words to words, subjects to subjects, verbs to verbs, phrases to phrases, or clauses to clauses.

Subordinating conjunctions also work to join. They can join clauses, but only clauses of unequal weight. They join a dependent clause to an independent clause.

If a clause starts with a subordinating conjunction, it's automatically a dependent clause. Reminder: A dependent clause standing alone is a sentence fragment. And that's what we want to master.

The following are examples of subordinating conjunctions:

after	even though	till
although	if	unless
as	if only	until
as if	in order that	when
as long as	once	whenever
as soon as	rather than	where
because	since	whereas
before	so that	whether
even if	though	while

Do you have to memorize these words? Absolutely not. If we think about these words, we find it's logical that what follows them must be connected to something else in order to make full sense.

Plus, a little familiarity goes a long way. Spending a few moments now getting to know these words will help you later as you edit your work to eliminate sentence fragments. You can think of these words as markers.

Here's a fragment that begins with a subordinating conjunction:

<u>Although</u> they were too tired to watch the movie.

The word *Although* is your clue! Right away, you're alerted to the possibility of a fragment. This fragment does have a subject, the word *they*, and a predicate, the word *were*. But something's missing.

What's missing is the information before or after the fragment. *Although* signals us that more information is required. The meaning of the clause depends on that information.

Here's another dependent clause sentence fragment:

<u>Whereas</u> my brother lives in a cold northern area.

The word *Whereas* is your clue. It kicks off a dependent clause. Like the previous example, this clause has a subject and a predicate, but the subordinating conjunction tells us the clause can't stand alone. It's dependent!

Solutions

There are two basic ways to correct these dependent clause fragments:

1. Join the dependent clause to an independent clause. With this solution, the independent clause holds the missing information:

    They stayed up past midnight <u>although</u> they were too tired to watch the movie.

    My sister lives in a warm region <u>whereas</u> my brother lives in a cold, northern area.

2. Remove the subordinating conjunction so the dependent clause becomes independent. Voilà! The fragment becomes a complete sentence:

    They were too tired to watch the movie.

    My brother lives in a cold northern area.

Tip

> A dependent clause can precede or follow an independent clause:
>
>> Even though her eyelids were heavy, she begged to skip her nap.
>>
>> She begged to skip her nap even though her eyelids were heavy.

Lesson 5: Fragment Clues: Relative Pronouns

We talked about pronouns back in Chapter 1. Now we're going to explore them further in relation to sentence fragments.

You know that pronouns step in for nouns. Examples of pronouns are *he, she, it, we*, and *they*. One group of pronouns is called *relative pronouns*. Relative pronouns function a little differently from other pronouns; they begin a clause and relate it to something else. The following are examples of relative pronouns:

- that
- whatever
- whichever
- whoever
- what

- which
- who
- whom
- whomever
- whose

Like subordinating conjunctions, relative pronouns can introduce a dependent clause. That means a relative pronoun can signal a fragment:

> <u>Whoever</u> is going to run in the race.

> <u>Whichever</u> you want to play!

These fragments seem like complete sentences, but they're lacking something. They don't include the person, idea, or thing to which they relate.

Solutions

We can correct this kind of sentence fragment by providing what's missing.

Each complete sentence below provides a relationship to the relative pronoun by connecting a related independent clause:

> **I will root** for <u>whoever</u> is going to run in the race.
> **We can play a game of your choice**, <u>whichever</u> you like best!

In these next solutions, we use another strategy. We turn the relative pronoun clause into a sentence subject and add a predicate:

> <u>Whoever is going to run in the race</u> **should sign** in now.
> <u>Whichever you like best</u> **is** the game I'm ready to play!

Lesson 6: Some Fragments Are Okay

Now that you know what sentence fragments may be missing—like a subject or a predicate—and what can signal a fragment—like a subordinating conjunction or a relative pronoun—let's look at when it's okay or even good to use a fragment.

Fragments can be okay in:

- advertising copy
- direct quotes
- dialogue
- informal writing
- anyplace you have intentionally used one for emphasis, style, or effect

It's good to be aware of your forum and your audience. What does this mean? Well, you'll want to consider what kind of writing you're creating and who will be reading it:

> Are you writing a dissertation? Fragments are a no-go there.

> Are you writing a letter to an old friend? Fragments could be fine, as long as your meaning is clear.

> Are you writing a short story? You might use fragments in your exposition or your dialogue.

You know the rules. You know what makes a sentence complete, and you can spot sentences that aren't complete. This means you can break the rules when appropriate in your own writing.

IN A NUTSHELL

You've covered a lot of ground by completing this chapter on sentence fragments.

Sentence fragments appear in all kinds of writing and are sometimes acceptable and even desirable for the effect they can produce. Most sentence fragments, however, are accidental and aren't grammatical. Fragments can detract from the flow, logic, and completeness of your thoughts.

Sentence fragments occur in writing in much the same way that measly serving of a single cherry presented itself while Aunt Felicity was slicing the pie.

While we're writing, our focus is often divided between what we were just thinking about and what we want to express next. Little pieces or incomplete thoughts get thrown between sentences. Though these pieces usually have a relationship to what precedes or follows them, they aren't complete or connected. The pie is the whole story we want to tell, and the slice of pie is a sentence from that story. We want to work on serving up a solid slice of pie.

Being able to detect fragments and understanding various ways to correct them will help you ensure your writing is as clear and thoughtful as possible.

In this chapter, you learned how to recognize sentence fragments, from short phrases to lengthy dependent clauses. And you've taken the next step by looking at ways to turn these fragments into complete sentences. You can add the missing component or join a fragment to an independent clause.

If you choose to use a fragment, then it will be an intelligent stylistic choice based on your knowledge of fragments and complete sentences.

FAQs

Q: What about a sentence like this? "That person is my friend." Is it a sentence fragment because it begins with a relative pronoun?

A: No, because in this case, the word *that* is not a relative pronoun; instead, it's an adjective modifying the word *person*. "That person" refers to a particular person. Reminder: Context determines what part of speech a word is.

Q: I thought words like *when* and *where* were adverbs, not subordinating conjunctions.

A: You're right that they're adverbs. But they're also conjunctions. Again, context is the determining factor for identifying parts of speech. When these words are working as conjunctions, some grammar guides call them *adverbial conjunctions*. By either name, adverbial or subordinating, they're conjunctions and can join a dependent clause to an independent one.

Chapter 5 Quiz

Question 1

Is the following a fragment or a complete sentence?

"Coconut whipped cream on your pie."

    a. fragment

    b. complete sentence

Question 2

Is the following a fragment or a complete sentence?

"Which one is your favorite?"

    a. fragment

    b. complete sentence

Question 3

Why should most sentence fragments be eliminated?

    a. to make your meaning clear and complete

    b. to speed up the flow of your writing

    c. to make your sentences long enough

Answer Key: Q1:a Q2:b Q3:a

CHAPTER 6

WHERE WE'LL STOP, NOBODY KNOWS

(run-on sentences)

Introduction

In this chapter, we'll look at run-on sentences and different ways to fix them. What's a run-on sentence? It's two or more independent clauses combined without adequate punctuation or conjunctions.

Imagine deciphering text that has little or no punctuation between sentences this would make your task as an intelligent reader difficult, tedious, or frustrating you would have to determine where to stop, where to pause, and where to go on without the guide of punctuation, or conjunctions, or capitalization to clue you in to the end of one sentence and the beginning of another one you might give up reading before you came to the end of the first paragraph you might muddle through however you could hoping that you were picking up the intended meaning.

Did you just find yourself unsure where to stop and start? Did you maybe even backtrack a few times? Readers need signals, and those signals are missing in the preceding paragraph.

When one idea runs into the next, we have to spend extra time and energy to figure out where a complete thought ends and another begins.

Readers don't have the drive to do all that work, and the trail of words they're struggling through can feel overwhelming or seem meaningless.

In a way, run-on sentences are the opposite of the sentence fragments you learned about in Chapter 5. While a fragment is an insufficient part of a sentence, a run-on sentence blends too many parts. A run-on is like a big, messy hunk of pie on your plate when you wanted one neat slice.

In this chapter, you're going to learn how to recognize run-ons, and then you'll try your hand at various ways of correcting them.

Lesson 1: Two Punctuation Fixes

In this lesson, we'll look at two punctuation options for eliminating *run-on sentences*:

- period
- semicolon

But first, how do you recognize a run-on?

Let's cleanse our palates after all that pie and try something light and refreshing: grapefruit.

To relish this healthy citrus fruit, you decide to prepare it the way a restaurant might serve it. You cut the grapefruit in half. Then, with a special serrated grapefruit knife, you saw through each little section of fruit to make perfect, triangular, bite-size pieces. All you have to do is scoop up a bite with your spoon and enjoy your grapefruit bite by bite... or so you think.

You find, however, that in your hurry to prepare this healthy snack designed to counteract the effects of eating too much pie, the bite-size pieces are still hanging together. You pick up not one little triangle in your spoon but two or even three.

Some of them are almost detached from their neighbors; others look like they haven't been sliced through at all. You're getting more than a mouthful. You need to do a better job with your serrated knife.

Think of each bite as an independent clause. Punctuation is about to come to the rescue. Punctuation is the writer's serrated knife. We can make a clean cut, or we can use punctuation more delicately to keep clauses connected when we really do want more than one bite at a time.

Let's analyze a run-on:

> You look in your <u>refrigerator, there's</u> that grapefruit you've been ignoring.

Notice how only a comma joins the two independent clauses. That's a grammar no-no. You may know this type of run-on by the name *comma splice*.

Here are the two independent clauses:

> Clause 1: You look in your refrigerator

> Clause 2: there's that grapefruit you've been ignoring

Now let's fix the problem!

Use a Period

As writers, we want to show where one complete thought ends.
A period is almost always a good solution:

> You look in your <u>refrigerator. There's</u> that
> grapefruit you've been ignoring.

We end the first clause with a period and start a new sentence
with a capital letter. We've solved the run-on problem by
creating two new sentences. Each is an independent clause that
can stand by itself.

Periods are full stops. They mark a firm separation
between sentences. When you use a period, your serrated knife
makes a clean cut.

Here's another run-on example:

> You tried to get one bite of grapefruit on your
> spoon you ended up with two bites.

This one's also made of two independent clauses. There's not
even a comma separating them. You may know this type of
run-on by the name *fused sentence*.

I call both varieties—comma splice and fused sentence—
run-on sentences.

We can use a period to fix it:

> You tried to get one bite of grapefruit on your
> <u>spoon. You</u> ended up with two bites.

Once again, we end the first clause with a period and start
a new sentence with a capital letter. We've solved the run-
on problem.

But you have options!

Use a Semicolon

Though we use the semicolon much less frequently than a period to fix a run-on, it's good for writers to have this punctuation mark in their back pockets. The semicolon can join two independent clauses that are relatively short in length and closely related in content.

The semicolon keeps a tight connection between the clauses.

PUNCTUATION NOTE

In this lesson, the rules you're learning apply to punctuation that joins independent clauses.

The punctuation we cover has other uses too, and we'll discuss those in an upcoming chapter.

Our sentence is a good candidate for the semicolon:

> You tried to get one bite of grapefruit on your spoon; you ended up with two bites.

The clauses are relatively short, and they're closely related. Here's another example with the semicolon:

> You wanted the two joined bites to be cleanly separated; you wanted two neat bites.

You have two punctuation options under your belt.

Lesson 2: More Punctuation Fixes

In this lesson, we'll look at how to eliminate run-on sentences with two more punctuation marks:

- colon
- dash

Announce with a Colon

We use the colon less frequently than the period or the semicolon, and it may be unfamiliar to you as a punctuation choice for connecting clauses. But the colon is an option.

Colons typically announce that something else is coming. This something else is going to tell you more about the first independent clause. When a colon joins two clauses, you can think of it as a megaphone. It announces additional, important information.

Here are a couple of example run-ons:

> Your determination kicked in, you silently pledged to get one bite of grapefruit on your spoon.

> A new thought motivates you grapefruit is easy to conquer.

And here the colon fixes them:

> Your determination kicked in: You silently pledged to get one bite of grapefruit on your spoon.

> A new thought motivates you: Grapefruit is easy to conquer.

Set Off with a Dash

The dash gives us one more way to use punctuation to fix a run-on.

The dash sets one clause apart from another.

Like the colon, the dash has a particular effect. It interrupts flow and creates emphasis on the second clause. This is something useful that we don't want to overdo.

Using the dash is like saying, "Oh, yeah, here's something else to pay attention to."

You want to be sure you intend to sidetrack your reader while calling attention to the clause that follows.

A dash can set off a second clause:

> At the stadium, french fries come in a giant plastic cup with a team logo—you've got to be sure to load them with catsup for the full taste experience!

We can also use a pair of dashes to set off a mid-sentence clause:

> The only two days of the year with no professional sports games—and I'm talking about MLB, NBA, NHL, and NFL games—are the day before and the day after the Major League Baseball All-Star Game.

As you experiment to fix run-ons, you can keep in mind the statement behind each punctuation mark:

- period = firm stop
- semicolon = tight connection
- colon = megaphone
- dash = set apart

Lesson 3: Comma Plus Coordinating Conjunction

You've met four punctuation marks that can fix run-ons. Now it's time to look at punctuation plus a conjunction.

The comma plus a coordinating conjunction can join two independent clauses.

Here are the coordinating conjunctions, which you met in previous lessons:

- and
- but
- for
- nor
- or
- so
- yet

Let's recycle a run-on sentence we worked with earlier to see what we can do with a comma plus a coordinating conjunction:

> You tried to get one bite of grapefruit on your spoon you ended up with two bites.

We can fix it like this, with a comma plus *but*:

> You tried to get one bite of grapefruit on your <u>spoon, but</u> you ended up with two bites.

Let's continue our story and try the comma plus other coordinating conjunctions:

> Two bites were more than you <u>wanted, so</u> you decided to use your serrated knife again.

> You hope your second attempt at dividing the triangular bites <u>works, or</u> you might decide to eat some pudding instead of the grapefruit.

When you encounter a run-on sentence, you can fix it by using a comma plus a coordinating conjunction between the independent clauses.

Why would you opt to use a comma plus a coordinating conjunction rather than use a period? Readers like familiarity, but they also like variety. If all sentences are the same length and the same structure, text gets dull. Short and to the point is good. But it can get tedious.

A period between the clauses will create two shorter sentences. A comma plus a coordinating conjunction will create one longer, flowing sentence.

The comma plus the coordinating conjunction allows you to vary the length and structure of your sentences. This method also allows you to create meaningful connections between your independent clauses.

CONJUNCTION NOTE

Just as there are subtle differences between the semicolon and the colon, there are some subtle differences between some of the coordinating conjunctions, between *but* and *yet*, and between *and* and *for*.

Lesson 4: The Semicolon Plus Rule

You learned in a previous lesson that the semicolon can join two relatively short, closely related clauses.

It's also possible to join two independent clauses with a semicolon plus a conjunctive adverb followed by a comma. Whew! That sounds much worse than it is. Let's call this the *semicolon plus* rule for short.

Right about now, I'm guessing you might want to know what a conjunctive adverb is.

I'll take you back to Chapter 1 and parts of speech for a moment to remind you that adverbs modify verbs, adjectives, and other adverbs. But that's not all! There's a subgroup of adverbs called conjunctive adverbs, and we use them to join clauses.

Here they are:

accordingly	finally	nevertheless
afterwards	furthermore	nonetheless
also	hence	otherwise
anyway	however	subsequently
besides	instead	therefore
certainly	likewise	thus
consequently	meanwhile	undoubtedly
conversely	moreover	

You can use a semicolon plus one of these conjunctive adverbs followed by a comma to correct run-on sentences (the semicolon plus rule).

How about a change of scene to see how the combo works? Here's a new run-on:

> The sea is midnight blue, the sky is azure blue.

Here the semicolon fixes it:

> The sea is midnight blue; the sky is azure blue.

Here the semicolon plus a conjunctive adverb plus a comma fixes it:

> The sea is midnight blue; however, the sky is azure blue.

Notice that the clause following the semicolon is an independent clause. It can stand alone, and it can stand alone even if you omit the conjunctive adverb:

> However, the sky is azure blue.

> The sky is azure blue.

Let's continue:

> The nighttime sky glistened with <u>stars: meanwhile, the</u> moon pulled the tides out to sea.

PUNCTUATION NOTE

Watch out for this ungrammatical construction:

The deep expanse of beach sat quiet and empty, nonetheless by morning it would be filled with sunbathers once again.

Many writers use conjunctive adverbs as if they were coordinating conjunctions. But when we join two independent clauses with a conjunctive adverb, we follow the semicolon plus rule:

> The deep expanse of nighttime beach sat quiet and <u>empty; nonetheless,</u> by morning it would be filled with sunbathers once again.

Lesson 5: Rewrite to Fix Run-Ons

So far, you've learned how to use punctuation or punctuation plus a conjunction to correct run-ons. Now let's look at different solutions, solutions that require some rewriting on your part, and maybe some creativity:

> You can make one of the clauses dependent on the other.

> You can transform the two independent clauses into one.

Make One Clause Dependent

You know something about dependent clauses from your work on fragments in Chapter 5. Now you can use that knowledge to correct run-ons.

To get a feel for the different effects of different methods, let's get back to the beach in the light of day:

The kids didn't want to put their swimsuits on, instead they jumped waves while still in their clothes.

Back on shore they warmed themselves in the sun, however clouds started to roll in.

Let's whip these run-ons into grammatical shape by rewriting. In both examples, we'll make one clause dependent by using a subordinating conjunction:

Since the kids didn't want to put their swimsuits on, they jumped waves while still in their clothes.

Back on shore they warmed themselves in the sun until clouds started to roll in.

You could rewrite each sentence many different ways. Using subordinating conjunctions allows you lots of flexibility in correcting run-ons.

Turn Two Clauses into One

Now let's rewrite by turning a run-on into one clause.

One of the sentences we were just working with is a good candidate for this method because the subject *kids* is responsible for the two predicates *didn't want* and *jumped*.

The kids didn't want to put their swimsuits on, they jumped waves while still in their clothes.

Let's rewrite it as one clause by using a conjunction to create a compound predicate. In the process, we'll eliminate the pronoun *they*:

> The <u>kids</u> <u>didn't want</u> to put their swimsuits on
> <u>and jumped</u> waves while still in their clothes.

Rewriting a run-on to make it one independent clause works best when the two clauses are closely related and have the same subject.

Let's continue rewriting run-ons:

> The sun looked as if it might never come back out
> it would be hiding for the rest of the day.
>
> Swimmers were discouraged by the weather, they
> began heading toward shore.

We'll transform the run-ons by giving each sentence one subject and a compound predicate:

> The <u>sun</u> <u>looked</u> as if it might never come back out
> <u>and would be hiding</u> for rest of the day.
>
> <u>Swimmers</u> <u>were discouraged</u> by the weather <u>and</u>
> <u>began heading</u> for shore.

You've soaked up a lot of information about run-on sentences!

IN A NUTSHELL

In this chapter, you worked with three different ways to fix run-on sentences:

- punctuation
- punctuation plus conjunction
- rewriting

You built on your grammar lexicon. You met four punctuation marks and used them to fix run-ons. You also learned more about adverbs (conjunctive adverbs), subordinating conjunctions, and dependent and independent clauses.

Some grammar rules are unambiguous: They dictate that there's a right way to do something, and any other way is wrong. But when it comes to fixing run-ons, there's almost always more than one solution.

All of us make mistakes when we set out to write or edit something. It's okay if at first you produce some run-on sentences. When you go back to check your work, you can fix any run-ons you discover. And you can fix them by selecting from the various methods you learned about in this chapter.

As you experiment with different ways to correct run-on sentences, you'll also be able to express your ideas more clearly. You can select punctuation marks and conjunctions, or you can use rewriting to create relationships between clauses.

Does this mean you should sweat every time you're faced with deciding between a period and a semicolon? Absolutely not. But it does mean you're equipped with the knowledge to make effective choices.

FAQs

Q: Can you clarify the difference between coordinating and subordinating conjunctions?

A: Conjunctions join one thing to another. Different kinds of conjunctions establish different kinds of connections between the two elements they join. Coordinate, as an adjective, means equal in rank or importance. Coordinating conjunctions join elements of equal importance. In the context of Chapter 6, these elements are independent clauses. Subordinate, as an adjective, means of inferior importance or rank. Subordinating conjunctions join a less important (or dependent) clause to a more important (or independent) one.

Q: Is it ever okay to use just a comma between independent clauses?

A: The comma by itself is conventionally accepted when it joins two very short clauses: You go first, they go second.

Q: Is there a rule for how many clauses can be in a sentence?

A: There's no rule, but the limits of reader comprehension can be your guide. Too many clauses joined together—even grammatically—can be tiring and confusing for your reader. Reading aloud will help you know if a very long sentence makes sense or would benefit from being divided into a few shorter sentences.

Chapter 6 Quiz

Question 1

Choose the run-on sentence.

    a. He was so excited to wake up on his birthday, he jumped right out of bed.

    b. He was so excited to wake up on his birthday that he jumped right out of bed.

    c. He was excited to wake up on his birthday, so he jumped right out of bed.

Question 2

Choose the run-on sentence.

    a. Waking up early has its perks: I was the first to get a cup of freshly brewed coffee.

    b. I was the first to get a cup of freshly brewed coffee waking up early has its perks

    c. Waking up early has its perks as I was the first to get a cup of freshly brewed coffee.

Question 3

A run-on sentence merges which of the following without including necessary punctuation?

    a. two or more subjects and a single predicate

    b. conjunctions with rewriting methods

    c. two or more independent clauses

Answer Key: Q1:a Q2:b Q3:c

CHAPTER 7

THEY WRITE, NOT WRITES, RIGHT?

(standard verb forms)

Introduction

Verbs. Have you ever heard that good writing revolves around them? Lots of writers and writing teachers believe it's true, and lots of people think verbs are the most difficult part of grammar.

In this lesson, we're going to shift gears, change the scene, get out of the kitchen for a while, and enter the big walk-in closet of verbs to do some serious browsing through the racks of clothes we'll find there. Verbs wear many different suits, and they change what they wear for lots of reasons.

For example, verbs change according to their subject: I *like* to swim and, perhaps, you and they *like* to swim, but the Portuguese water dog *likes* to swim. Do you notice how the word *like* becomes *likes* when the subject is *Portuguese water dog*?

Verbs also change according to when their action takes place. For example, today you *swim*, but yesterday you *swam*. The word *swim* becomes *swam* when it took place yesterday.

Even more factors affect verbs. Does a single subject or a plural subject make the verb happen? Is what's happening real or imaginary? Is it active or passive?

In this chapter, we'll explore some of the essential ideas that shape verbs. We'll cover the rules for regular verbs, and we'll also take note of irregular verbs—verbs that don't follow the usual rules.

Five ideas affect verbs:

- person
- number
- tense
- voice
- mood

These are words you probably know, but each has a special meaning in grammar. We'll give definition to these words and then see how the ideas they represent affect verbs.

Even when we're not conscious of it, we always use person, number, tense, voice, and mood to shape verbs. Let's find out what they are!

Lesson 1: Person and Number

Person and number are a duo that work together to give shape to verbs.

(In an upcoming lesson, you'll see how person and number also shape agreement and consistency in your writing.)

We'll start with a look at person:

Person	Number	
	Singular	Plural
First person	I	we
Second person	you	you
Third person	he/she/it	they

That's a bunch of pronouns. Let's put them into action!

Imagine you're in front of an audience.

You're a storyteller. You could be speaking to a real audience, or you could be writing for a reading audience. To your audience you say (or write):

> **I** want to tell you a story.
>
> > I = person speaking = first person singular

Now, imagine you're working with a group of storytellers. Together, you say:

> **We** want to tell you a story.
>
> > We = group speaking = first person plural

You've probably figured out that number, as applied to verbs, means singular (one) or plural (more than one).

Now, imagine you'd like someone else to tell a story.

You could speak directly to one of your fellow storytellers and say:

> **You** tell the story, please.
>
> > You = second person singular = the person
> > spoken to.

You could speak to several of the storytellers and say:

> **You** take over the story, please.
>
> > You = second person plural = the people
> > spoken to.

✎ **Tip** _____

> While most languages have different words for *you*
> singular and *you* plural, English has only one word
> for both: *you*. We understand from context if *you* is
> singular or plural.

Finally, you decide to tell a story about other people. You narrate what someone else is doing:

> **He** tells a story.
>
> **She** tells a story.
>
> **It** tells a story.
>
>> He/she/it = third person singular = person or thing spoken about.
>
> **They** tell a story.
>
>> They = third person plural = people or things spoken about.

Let's further establish your understanding of person.

First and second person can only be pronouns—*I, we, you* singular, and *you* plural.

Third person can be a pronoun—*he, she, it,* or *they.* Or third person can be a noun.

Lesson 2: Tense, Voice, and Mood

Tense

In relation to verbs, tense means time. Tense gives verbs their place in history (past), in the now (present), and in what will be (future).

Tense can be simple or complex. In this book, we'll concentrate on the *simple tenses*. You'll also get a little preview of *complex tenses*.

We categorize tense this way:

- past (We **iced** the cake an hour ago.)
- present (We **ice** the cake now.)
- future (We **will ice** the cake later.)

Voice

Voice is either *active* or *passive*.

When the subject makes the verb happen, the voice is active:

> The **dog walker walks** the dog.

When the verb is happening to the subject, the voice is passive:

> The **dog is walked** daily by the dog walker.

Active voice makes writing dynamic. But careful, deliberate use of passive voice can be effective. It can emphasize the passive role of the subject:

The evil **teacher hit** the boy. (active)

The poor, helpless **boy was hit** by the teacher. (passive)

Mood

In human emotions, there are many moods. In grammar, there are three:

- indicative (for making statements and asking questions)
- imperative (for issuing orders)
- subjunctive (for wishing, supposing, or imagining)

The indicative mood is straightforward. It's the mood we naturally use for statements or questions. Here are a few examples:

He's her brother. (indicative statement, also called a *declarative*)

Are they related to you? (indicative question, also called an *interrogative*)

We use the imperative mood for issuing orders and making commands. This mood often calls for an exclamation point. Back in Chapter 4, you learned that in imperative sentences, the subject *you* is often implied rather than stated:

[You] Put your napkin on your lap!

[You] Be sure to get to school on time.

We use the subjunctive for imagining and wishing, and for the hypothetical.

The following words and phrases can be clues to this mood:

- as if
- as though
- could
- if

- might
- should
- would

The subjunctive mood requires us to use some verb forms that might seem peculiar:

> She wishes **she were** an expert predictor
> of earthquakes.

> If only **he were** a more adventurous person, he
> would join the ice-climbing expedition.

The sentences above show how the subjunctive mood can change our usual verb form.

In the indicative, we partner the word *he*, *she*, *or it* with the word *was*:

> **She was** an expert predictor of earthquakes.

But in the subjunctive, we partner the words *he*, *she*, *or it* with the word *were*:

> He could be an expert if **he were** able to
> take more classes and gain more on-the-
> job experience.

Don't worry if you're thinking, *Uh-oh, this seems wrong*. The unfamiliar can seem wrong at first.

✍ Tip _____

Here are two things to note about the subjective mood:

1. The odd verbs in the subjunctive are grammatically correct.

2. While it's good for you to recognize the existence of the subjunctive mood and understand it, you're not required to use it.

_____

Lesson 3: Verb Power

Did your old English teacher Mr. Gray ever take his red pen to your papers and circle your verbs?

Let's go with the premise that verbs are the main force propelling a piece of writing.

We'll use a short poem to bring verbs into focus.

> Clouds
>
> White sheep, white sheep,
> On a blue hill,
> When the wind stops,
> You all stand still.
> When the wind blows,
> You walk away slow.
>
> White sheep, white sheep,
>
> Where do you go?
>
> (—Anonymous)

This little poem has six verbs:

- stops
- stand
- blows
- walk
- do
- go

Five of them are main verbs. That means they can work alone as the predicate in a sentence. One is a helping verb. (More on this is coming up soon!)

Regular and Irregular Verbs

Out of the six verbs, two are *regular* and four—or nearly 67 percent—are *irregular*. (I'm stretching my math skills here.) This sampling may not be typical. But it's true that English has many irregular verbs.

If you've ever studied a foreign language, then you've probably conjugated a verb, or taken it through its different forms. In English, regular verbs follow a uniform pattern. That's what makes them regular.

Irregular verbs deviate from that pattern.

Next up, we'll explore the uniform pattern and the deviations to understand more about regular and irregular verbs.

Lesson 4: The Simple Tenses

To further explore verbs, we need to add the idea of *tense* to the ideas of person and number.

We'll begin at the beginning...

Every verb has a starting place. We call that the base form. You can think of home base. That's where a batter starts when it's their turn up at bat!

The base form is the main entry you'll find in the dictionary. We add endings to the base form according to person, number, and tense. You may know this as *conjugating* a verb.

Let's track one regular verb and one irregular verb through their different forms as determined by person, number, and tense.

First we'll use the verb *stop* to demonstrate regular verb forms.

And then we'll use the verb *blow* to demonstrate irregular verb forms.

Here's regular verb *stop*:

Person and Number	Present Tense	Past Tense	Future Tense
First person singular I	stop	stopped	will stop
Second person singular you	stop	stopped	will stop
Third person singular he/she/it	stops	stopped	will stop
First person plural we	stop	stopped	will stop
Second person plural you	stop	stopped	will stop
Third person plural they	stop	stopped	will stop

✍ **Tip** _____

Basics to note about standard verb forms:

1. Past tense verbs take an *ed* ending. (Spelling rules tell us when to double the consonant before adding *ed*.)

2. Future tense verbs use helping verb *will*.

3. Third person singular present tense verbs take an *s* ending. This may seem baffling because for nouns, the addition of an *s* makes a plural. But for verbs, an *s* ending means third person singular, present tense.

_____

Now let's look at irregular verb *blow*:

Person and Number	Present Tense	Past Tense	Future Tense
First person singular I	blow	blew	will blow
Second person singular you	blow	blew	will blow
Third person singular he/she/it	blows	blew	will blow
First person plural we	blow	blew	will blow
Second person plural you	blow	blew	will blow
Third person plural they	blow	blew	will blow

1. Irregular verbs don't take an *ed* ending for past tense. They do something else. In the case of irregular verb *blow*, the vowel changes from *o* to *e*. Other verbs do other things. For example, *drink* becomes *drank*.

2. Fortunately, you have an easy resource to assist you when you're unsure of an irregular verb. You can find the past form for irregular verbs in most dictionaries. Some dictionaries will simply list the word, some will note it as *past*, and some will note it as *inflected form*.

Ready for more? Let's meet the perfect tenses.

Lesson 5: The Perfect Tenses

So far, we've explored simple tense verbs. That's what we use most of the time to express concepts of past, present, and future.

Sometimes, however, we need to refine our expression of time, and for doing that, we use the *perfect tenses*. Their name makes sense if we think of them as verbs that help us more *perfectly* pinpoint an action in time.

The perfect tenses are excellent for specifying when something occurred in relation to something else. I like to think of the perfect tenses as defining a time preceding a later time.

To understand these tenses, we're going to add *past participle* to your grammar lexicon. It's important to understand the past participle so you can be sure you're using the right verb forms in your writing.

Let's show it in a verb table:

Base Form	Present	Past	Future	Past Participle
sigh	sigh/sighs	sighed	(will) sigh	(had, has/have, will have) sighed
blow	blow/blows	blew	(will) blow	(had, has/have, will have) blown

Now let's get to the question of what's a participle.

It's a verb form that helps us express more tenses, but it can't stand alone. It needs help! We help it by adding a helping verb.

✍ Tip

1. Regular verbs use the same word for the simple past tense and the past participle (stopped, stopped). Irregular verbs often use different words for the past tense and the past participle (ex: blew, blown).

2. The perfect tenses partner a past, present, or future form of the verb *have* with a past participle. The tense of the helping verb determines past, present, or future perfect tense!

3. A good dictionary will include both the past and the participle forms of irregular verbs.

How to Make Perfect Tense Verbs

There's a formula to follow to make the perfect tenses. We use a form of helping verb *have* plus the *past participle* of our main verb:

- past perfect = had + past participle of main verb
- present perfect = have or has (third person singular) + past participle of main verb
- future perfect = will have + past participle of main verb

Here they are in action:

Past perfect:

Yesterday and the day before, he took a walk at noon, but today he **had** already **walked** before he **ate** breakfast.

(The past perfect **had walked** occurred in a time before the simple past **ate** occurred.)

Present perfect:

I **want** to skip my noon walk. I **have walked** already.

(The present perfect **have walked** has occurred before the simple present tense **want** occurs.)

Future perfect:

They **will have walked** by the time you **will put** your shoes on to take your walk.

(Did you guess that the future perfect **will have walked** will occur in a time before the simple future tense **will put** will occur?)

✍ Tip

> If we use the past participle alone, it's not a complete predicate.
>
> This sentence is ungrammatical because it uses only a past participle, not a complete verb:
>
> The wind **blown**.
>
> How do we complete the verb? We add a helping verb:
>
> The wind **has blown**.

Do we need to use the perfect tenses? Most of the time, we can use the simple tenses. They locate us on the timeline of past, present, and future. We put the perfect tenses to work when we need to show fine differences in story-telling timelines.

IN A NUTSHELL

I'm guessing that you've had your fill of verbs. The good news is that you've covered a lot of ground.

You learned how to use standard verb forms by applying the five ideas that shape verbs:

- person
- number
- tense
- voice
- mood

We can think of each of the five ideas as part of a suit—let's say a tie, shirt, jacket, skirt or pants, and the style. In combination, they make the whole suit, or the standard verb forms.

You learned the basics about main verbs and helping verbs, and you've begun to explore some of the more complex verb forms.

With the foundation work in this lesson, you can consciously select standard verb forms. You have the ability to establish consistency in your writing— especially in person, number, and tense. And you'll be able to apply this knowledge as you go on to matters of agreement between subjects, verbs, and pronouns.

You can also elect to alter the mood and voice in your writing, thereby creating emphasis and variety in your work.

Next lesson, we're moving out of the suit closet. Go ahead and loosen your tie and kick off your shoes after a hard day's work.

Q: I thought a participle was an adjective, not a verb?

A: That's right! A participle is a verb form that can act as a verb. Or it can act as an adjective. Here are examples with the verb *deplete*:

> **Past participle as adjective:** After twelve hours in the library, the intellectually *depleted* student took a two-hour nap.

> **Past participle as the complement of a linking verb:** The student felt *depleted*.

> **Present participle as the kick-off to a modifying phrase:** *Depleting* his power of thinking by studying too much, the student didn't get to sleep until four hours after his usual bedtime.

Q: How can I figure out the base form of a verb when I want to look up irregular past and past participles?

A: Many dictionaries will lead you to the base form. For example, if you look up *is*, a good dictionary will lead you to base form *be*.

Chapter 7 Quiz

Question 1

Name the verb tense in the following sentence: "Detective X had investigated more than 177 mysteries by 2012."

    a. future perfect

    b. future

    c. past perfect

Question 2

Which person would be a match for a present tense verb with an *s* ending? (Example: talks.)

    a. third person plural

    b. third person singular

    c. second person singular or plural

Question 3: In most writing, which voice is best to use most of the time?

    a. active

    b. argumentative

    c. passive

Answer Key: Q1:c Q2:b Q3:a

CHAPTER 8

YOU ARE YOU

(pronouns)

Introduction

KEYWORDS:

◊ pronoun   ◊ complement

◊ antecedent   ◊ modifier

◊ subject   ◊ object

Are you wondering why you're about to be immersed in pronouns? There's more to pronouns than what you've seen so far. In some ways, pronouns are as vast a topic as verbs because, like verbs, they have so many different forms. That's why we're devoting an entire chapter to them.

In this chapter, we'll explore eight pronoun groups. We'll focus on the *personal pronouns*, and you'll get an overview of seven other types.

We'll travel through a virtual pronoun cafeteria line!

Along the way, you'll learn how to determine a pronoun's proper form in a sentence depending on its role as:

- subject
- complement
- object

Pronouns perform a surprising number of jobs. They can do all of the following:

- step in for nouns
- determine who's speaking to or about whom
- modify other parts of speech
- show ownership
- work like mirrors and reflect

- act upon a verb or be acted upon by a verb
- show intensity
- identify members of a group without being quantitatively specific

In everyday writing, lots of pronoun errors occur. You're going to learn how to use the right pronouns, and this will help ensure your writing is clear.

Lesson 1: The Person in Personal Pronouns

You met an important group of pronouns in the previous chapter. They're called *personal pronouns*. Let's start with them as we explore the different uses of pronouns.

Singular			Plural		
First person singular	Second person singular	Third person singular	First person plural	Second person plural	Third person plural
I	you	he/she/it	we	you	they

Here's a quick re-refresher:

- First person = the speaker (or writer)
- Second person = the person spoken to
- Third person = the person spoken about

Each of these personal pronouns can stand on its own as the subject of a sentence. And each can step in for nouns or other pronouns.

When a pronoun steps in, we call the word or phrase it replaces the *antecedent* or *referent*. I'll stick with the term *antecedent*, but if you see the term *referent* in other grammar guides, you'll know it means the same thing.

The prefix *ante-* means *earlier* or *before*. You can connect that definition to the role of the noun or pronoun that a pronoun steps in for. Conceptually, the antecedent comes before the pronoun.

Usually, the antecedent makes an appearance in a sentence before its pronoun does, but sometimes the pronoun makes an appearance before its antecedent:

> The <u>boy</u> ate his vegetables because <u>he</u> had to in order to get dessert.
>
> Because <u>he</u> had to in order to get dessert, the <u>boy</u> ate his vegetables.

In the sentences above, the word *boy* is the antecedent, and the word *he* is the pronoun.

Subject and Complement Pronouns

I'm confident that you know about sentence subjects.

Here are pronouns acting as subjects:

> <u>They</u> have never eaten in a cafeteria.
>
> Do <u>you</u> enjoy cafeteria-style restaurants?
>
> <u>She</u> has never been to an eatery like that.

Let's add to your grammar lexicon and define *complement*. To do that, we need to call on your understanding of verbs, linking verbs in particular.

Linking verbs set up a connection between what's on one side (the subject) and what's on the other side (the complement). They work like an equal sign.

A complement is the *completion* of a linking verb. As a matter of fact, *complement* and *completion* have in common their first six letters: *c-o-m-p-l-e*.

Let's break down a couple of sentences that follow this structure: subject-linking verb-complement:

Mr. Gray is a teacher.

Mr. Gray = subject

is = linking verb

teacher = complement

Aunt Felicity feels happiness when she bakes.

Aunt Felicity = subject

feels = linking verb

happiness = complement

When pronouns work as complements, they're in the same form as subject pronouns! But many writers don't get this right. Now you can.

Let's add subject and complement pronouns:

Person and Number	Subject and Complement Pronouns
First person singular	I
Second person singular	you
Third person singular	he/she/it
First person plural	we
Second person plural	you
Third person plural	they

Each of these sentence examples has a pronoun acting as a complement:

> Mr. Gray is <u>he</u>.
>
> The girl is <u>she</u>.
>
> The student is <u>you</u>.

These next sentence examples emphasize that a pronoun takes the same form whether it's a subject or a complement:

> <u>You</u> are <u>you</u>.
>
> <u>They</u> are <u>they</u>.
>
> <u>He</u> is <u>he</u>.

The truth is, pronoun grammar like this is disappearing from our everyday writing. In informal speaking and writing, you may not want to follow the rules. But it's good to know them; they still hold in formal writing.

✍ Tip

Is it me or I, her or she, him or he?

When you pick up the phone and the caller says, "I'd like to speak to Margo LaFonda," and you're Margo LaFonda, your grammatically correct response is: "This is she."

If this sounds haughty or pretentious, overly formal, or plain old wrong to you, that's probably because we don't often hear this grammatically correct use of a pronoun complement.

Lack of familiarity makes what's right sound off-putting. "This is her" sounds more acceptable because we're more accustomed to it. But what sounds right isn't always grammatically correct. It's up to you how grammatical you want to be!

Of course, you have an alternative. You can answer, "I'm Margo."

Now you're ready for some pronoun pairing.

Lesson 2: Compounds and Partners

When we use a pronoun as part of a compound subject, the rules of grammar dictate that the pronoun be in subject form:

> <u>Mark Black and I</u> are going to the movies.

> Mark Black and I = compound subject

> <u>She and her siblings</u> will meet at a great coffee house after the movie.

> She and her siblings = compound subject

The words *I* and *she* are part of their respective sentence subjects, so they must be in subject form.

Noun Partners as Subjects

Sometimes the personal pronouns are partnered with a subject noun. And when they are, they should be in subject form.
Example noun partners:

> <u>We marathon runners</u> need to hydrate frequently.

> We marathon runners = partners

> <u>You students</u> should take a break after so much intensive studying.

> You students = partners

Object Pronouns

You're ready for another pronoun form. Let's add *object pronouns*:

Person and Number	Subject and Complement Pronouns	Object Pronouns
First person singular	I	me
Second person singular	you	you
Third person singular	he/she/it	him/her/it
First person plural	we	us
Second person plural	you	you
Third person plural	they	them

(Note that pronouns *you* and *it* stay the same, whether acting as subject or object.)

Pronouns take the object form when they are:

- the object of a transitive verb
- the object of a preposition

We can return to our mixed-up verbs *lie* and *lay* for a moment to explain *transitive verbs* versus *intransitive verbs*.

Lie is an intransitive verb. Its action is complete; it doesn't need to act upon something:

> You lie down to rest. (The verb doesn't take an object.)

Lay is a transitive verb. Its action is complete when it's performed on something:

> I lay my head in my hands. (The verb takes an object, *head*.)

Let's apply this concept of object to pronouns. Pronouns take the object form when they're the object of a verb or the object of a preposition:

Object of a verb:

> The Frisbee <u>hit her</u>.
>
> I <u>passed them</u> on the highway.

Object of a preposition:

> Give the Frisbee <u>to her</u>.
>
> Save some potatoes <u>for me</u>, please.

Note that pronouns *you* and *it* stay the same, whether acting as subject or object.

Compound Objects

Just as there are compound subjects that include a pronoun, there are compound objects that include a pronoun.

When pronouns are part of a compound object, they should be in object form:

> The Frisbee almost <u>hit your sister and me</u> as it sailed by.
>
> Pass the potatoes again, please, <u>to Mom and us</u> down at this end of the table.

Noun Partners as Objects

And, you may have guessed, there are noun partner objects that include a pronoun:

> How about offering some of that coffee to <u>us students</u>?

> The waves sprayed <u>us shell seekers</u> as we walked along the shoreline.

Lesson 3: Possessive Pronouns

We're going to look at the personal pronoun list one more time, with one additional group: possessive pronouns and modifiers.

Person and Number	Subject and Complement Pronouns	Object Pronouns	Possessive Pronouns and Modifiers
Third person singular	he/she/it	him/her/it	his/hers/its/her
First person plural	we	us	ours/our
Second person plural	you	you	yours/your
Third person plural	they	them	theirs/their

Some of these possessives can stand alone as subjects, objects, or complements, while others serve as *modifiers* and can't stand alone. (Reminder: Modifiers tell us more about something. For example, adjectives are modifiers that tell us about nouns.)

All possessive pronouns work to show what belongs to whom.

Possessives as Modifiers

We use this group of possessive pronouns to modify nouns in the same way that adjectives do:

- my
- his
- its
- yours

- whose
- her
- our
- their

Example possessives as modifiers:

<u>My</u> dress was expensive.

<u>Your</u> old tennis balls have lost their bounce.

We can also partner these pronouns with *gerunds*. A gerund is an *ing* verb form that works as a noun:

<u>His going</u> out to play tennis means we can't go to the movies.

<u>My wishing</u> for something will make it happen.

Possessives as Subject, Complement, or Object

These possessives can stand by themselves:

- mine
- his/hers/its
- theirs
- yours
- our
- whose

These pronouns keep the same form whether they're working as subject, complement, or object. (Note that the words *his* and *its* stay the same in stand-alone or modifier form.)

Example possessives as subject, complement, or object:

<u>Yours</u> is lost! (subject)

That basketball ball is <u>mine</u>! (complement)

Please return <u>hers</u> to the hopper. (object)

You've met the personal pronouns as subject, complement, object, and possessive. You have seven more groups of pronouns to meet!

Lesson 4: More Pronouns

Relative Pronouns

You might recall your introduction to this next pronoun group from Chapter 5, when we looked at clues to sentence fragments. They are the relative pronouns:

- that
- whatever
- whichever
- whoever

- whomever
- what
- which

- who
- whom
- whose

Here's a quick refresher on what we've already covered in understanding the role of relative pronouns: They link and relate a dependent clause to that which precedes or follows it:

> Having no homework over the holiday is a perk <u>that</u> makes most students happy.

The word "relate" will help you remember what these pronouns do.

 **Tip**

> We use relative pronouns based on the word *who* to refer to people and sometimes animals.
>
>> The student <u>who</u> is taking this course is self-motivated.
>
>> To <u>whom</u> does the book belong?
>
> We use relative pronoun *that* to refer to things and sometimes animals:
>
>> The chair <u>that</u> is upside down is broken.
>
>> The squid <u>that</u> is hiding won't be caught.
>
> (Some grammar guides say *that* is also for humans and other animals.)

Pronouns based on the word *who* often cause confusion. These rules should help you keep them straight:

The words *who* and *whoever* are subject pronouns.

> Whoever wants to go to the cafeteria for lunch should meet by the elevators at noon.

The words *whom* and *whomever* are object pronouns.

> Because the patron doesn't like coleslaw, she asks the server to give it to whomever he serves next.

Interrogative Pronouns

These pronouns are used to ask questions:

- what
- which
- who
- whose

Interrogative means *question*. Keeping that in mind should help you remember what these pronouns do.

You may have noticed that the interrogative pronouns are also in the relative pronoun group. Their role changes according to what they're doing in a sentence.

Example sentences with interrogative pronouns:

> What do you mean?
>
> Which did you choose?
>
> Who will be the first?
>
> Whose are those?

Indefinite Pronouns

The pronouns in this group don't require an antecedent. They can stand on their own:

- all
- any
- both
- either
- many
- neither
- no one
- other
- some
- something
- another
- anything
- each
- few
- most
- nobody
- one
- several
- someone

Though they can stand on their own, they're vague. We can't pinpoint exactly to what or to whom or to how many they refer:

> <u>Anyone</u> planning on going, please raise your hand. (We don't know what people or how many.)
>
> <u>Some</u> of the desserts look homemade! (We don't know exactly which ones.)

To remember what these pronouns do, you can associate their name *indefinite* to its meaning of *not precise* or *vague*.

Lesson 5: Even More Pronouns

The following pronouns can be reflexive or intensive, depending on what they're doing in a sentence:

- herself
- itself
- ourself
- yourself
- himself
- myself
- themselves
- yourselves

Reflexive Pronouns

Reflexive pronouns mirror their subject. You can associate the word *mirror* with the term *reflexive*, which means turned back on itself.

They can be objects or complements, but they don't work as subjects. Let's look at some examples:

> She likes <u>herself</u>. (*Herself* reflects *she*.)

> The boy poked <u>himself</u> in the eye. (*Himself* reflects *boy*.)

> The patients are not feeling like <u>themselves</u> today. (*Themselves* reflects *patients*.)

The following sentence demonstrates a common mistake:

> The girl and <u>myself</u> like to jump rope.

Can you tell why the reflexive pronoun *myself* doesn't belong? It has nothing to reflect!

Drawing from your pronoun knowledge, you can determine that the subject pronoun form is correct. You can test this by removing the other subject:

> ~~The girl and~~ I like to jump rope.

Intensive Pronouns

These pronouns are used for extra emphasis or intensity, as their name indicates. We use them to give a little extra oomph to a subject:

> I, <u>myself</u>, don't like beets.

> The author, <u>himself</u>, is responsible for every single word of the text.

An intensive pronoun can be omitted without changing the basic intent of a sentence.

> I don't like beets.

> The author is responsible for every single word of the text.

Demonstrative Pronouns

Like the indefinite pronouns, the demonstrative pronouns don't require an antecedent:

- that
- these
- this
- those

The words *this* and *that* are singular, while the words *these* and *those* are plural.

The words *this* and *these* are for the nearest thing or things, while the words *that* and *those* are for a more distant thing or things.

The demonstrative pronouns can stand alone, or they can act as modifiers:

> <u>These</u> are perfectly roasted beans. (stand-alone pronoun)
>
> <u>This</u> coffee bean is perfectly roasted. (modifier)

They work to identify something much like a pointer, either literally or theoretically. Take a look at these examples:

> Give her <u>those</u> pieces.
>
> <u>That</u> is the way I like my coffee.

You can associate the word *demonstrate* with this pronoun group.

Reciprocal Pronouns

This is a small pronoun group:

- each other
- one another

These word pairs work together, with something being passed between them—literally or figuratively. *Reciprocate* means *give and take mutually*.

Here are a few examples:

The guinea pigs nosed <u>one another</u>.

The lovebirds kissed <u>each other</u>.

The cafeteria staff have worked with <u>one another</u> for several years and have a good system.

Conventionally, we use *one another* for more than two people or things and *each other* for just two people or things. But these are loose rules and not everyone follows them.

IN A NUTSHELL

Were you surprised to discover we have so many pronouns and that they're used in so many different ways?

In this chapter, you saw that pronouns do a lot more than step in for nouns.

Pronouns keep us from repeating ourselves in a tedious fashion. We can compare the following two short paragraphs:

Ms. Francesca finished a good book yesterday. Ms. Francesca wanted to tell the students in the third-grade class that Ms. Francesca teaches that the book is now one of her favorites.

Ms. Francesca finished a good book yesterday. She wanted to tell her third-grade students that the book is now one of her favorites.

While it retains meaning, the second paragraph is shorter, more concise, and less repetitive than the first paragraph.

Pronouns represent people and things—specific and not specific—they reflect, they add emphasis, they show ownership, they figuratively point to something, they ask questions, they relate one clause to another, they give further definition to people, places, and things, and they show who or what is executing an action and who or what is being acted upon.

With their many roles and forms, pronouns also serve an important part in keeping your meaning clear and precise.

You learned how to use the right pronoun, depending on its role in a sentence. This will help you avoid some common grammar errors.

You've come to the end of this pronoun cafeteria line.

After all the work you've accomplished in this lesson, you're ready for the next goal, which is to ensure your intended meaning is evident lucidly and grammatically as you put together your subjects, verbs, and pronouns. All that is just ahead in Chapter 9!

FAQs

Q: Which pronoun should I use when I don't know the gender of the antecedent?

A: The trend is for writers to avoid using gender-specific pronouns. The old solutions were to use *he or she*, *he/she* each time, or to alternate between *he* and *she* throughout. Today, those strategies don't meet the standards and goals for inclusivity. The use of *they/them/their*—which we used to reserve for plurals—in place of *his or her* (singular) has become more and more acceptable... but not to everybody everywhere. Sometimes, writers change a singular subject to a plural, and then they can use plural pronouns *they/them/their*. And still others work with the pronoun *one* to resolve this dilemma. (The use of *one*, however, is fairly formal.) These are stylistic and sometimes political choices. Try reading your work aloud to see what works best for you. And if you're working for a publication, be in touch with its preferred style guide.

Q: In a sentence like the example below, is the pronoun a subject or an object?

Give the directions to whoever/whomever wants to go.

A: Sometimes a subject seems like an object. At first glance, it looks like *whoever* is the object of the preposition *to*. In fact, it is the subject of the clause *whoever wants to go*. You need to look at the whole sentence to discover the pronoun's true role. The pronoun's role as subject of its own clause supersedes its role as object of the preposition, making *whoever* correct.

Q: Are the words *which* and *that* interchangeable?

A: You'll get different answers from different authorities on this one, but I'll offer my guidelines.

Use the word *that* when it begins a clause that is absolutely essential to limiting what precedes it (also called a *restrictive clause*). Here's an example:

> Give your money to the charity <u>that</u> is
> most in need.

Use the word *which* when the clause that follows provides additional but not absolutely essential information (also called a *nonrestrictive clause*). Here's an example:

> He returned your cake pan, <u>which</u> he had
> promised to do.

This distinction between restrictive and nonrestrictive clauses will come up again when we look at punctuation in a later chapter. Notice in the examples above that there's no comma before *that*, but there is a comma before *which*.

Chapter 8 Quiz

Question 1

Which is a possessive pronoun?

   a. they

   b. mine

   c. it's

Question 2

Which would be right as an object partner?

   a. us bakers

   b. we bakers

   c. they bakers

Question 3

What's ungrammatical in the following sentence?

"They invited my whole family and myself to the movie premiere!"

   a. Pronoun *They* should be *Them*.

   b. Pronoun *myself* should be *me*.

   c. Pronoun *my* should be *mine*.

Answer Key: Q1:b Q2:a Q3:b

CHAPTER 9

LET'S AGREE TO AGREE

(agreement: subjects and verbs, pronouns and antecedents)

Introduction

It's time to apply what you've learned about subjects, verbs, and pronouns to see how these three get along with one another in a variety of sentence constructions. In this chapter, you'll learn about agreement between subjects and verbs and between pronouns and their antecedents.

We're going back to the cafeteria line! Imagine you've selected all your food, the dishes are on your tray, and you've paid the cashier. Before you sit down to dig into your meal, you head over to a station to select your supplies.

You can choose from cutlery, condiments, napkins, straws, swizzle sticks, and packets of salt, pepper, and sugar. What goes with the meal you chose? You do a quick analysis of the items on your tray. If you ordered a veggie burger, you might need an extra napkin because the secret sauce is messy. If you chose hot tea and you like it sweet, you'll want a packet or two of sugar. A spoon would be useful for a dessert like a double scoop of mango sorbet. The items you choose should agree with your meal.

In this chapter—much in the same way you analyzed the contents of your tray to figure out if you need a fork or spoon, lemon or sugar, mustard or catsup, one napkin or five—we're going to analyze the contents of our sentences to figure out what we might need to do to ensure agreement.

Lesson 1: Subject-Verb Agreement

Agreement means sentence parts are in harmony. We're going to look at several kinds of sentence subjects to match them with the right verb:

- collective nouns
- compound subjects that represent a single unit
- *each* and *every* as a compound
- plural forms with a singular concept
- plural forms with a plural concept

You'll meet some clear rules, and you'll meet some rules that depend on your interpretation of what a sentence intends to say.

Collective Nouns

Collective nouns are words that name a group. Here's
a sampling:

- audience
- band
- cast
- committee
- crowd

- family
- flock
- group
- lot

These group words usually work with a singular verb form
but occasionally with a plural verb form, depending on
the sentence.

When the group operates as a unit, the collective noun
partners with a singular verb form:

> The <u>flock flies</u> south.
>
> The birds unite in their flight pattern. We think of
> them as a unit.

When group members operate as separate individuals, the
collective noun partners with a plural verb form:

> At the sound of thunder, the <u>flock panic</u> and fly in
> many directions.

(Just about now, a little reminder might come in handy.
Remember those verb tables from Chapter 7? Present tense,
third person singular verbs end in *s*. Third person plural verbs
don't end in *s*.)

Let's look at two more examples to understand the correct verb form:

1. A <u>lot needs</u> to be cleaned up.

In that sentence, the word *lot* is a collective noun working as a singular concept, so the verb form is singular.

2. A <u>lot need</u> to be printed again because the client wants color brochures.

In that sentence, the word *lot* is a collective noun representing multiple things that are operating independently, so the verb form is plural.

 **Tip**

If you're having any trouble determining if a group word is singular or plural, try a logical substitution for the collective noun. This method can help you make sense of the subject-verb agreement. Take a look at these example sentences:

Singular: A <u>lot needs</u> to be cleaned up. A <u>large chunk needs</u> to be cleaned up.

Plural: A <u>lot need</u> to be printed again because the client wants color brochures. <u>Many pages need</u> to be printed again because the client wants color brochures.

Compound Subjects That Represent a Single Unit

You know that when we join two subjects with the word *and*, the result is a *compound subject*. The conjunction *and* works like a plus sign, making one subject plus another into a plural subject that requires a plural verb form:

> The student and the teacher work well together.

But there are exceptions to the basic rule. Some compound subjects are thought of as so closely connected that together they make a new whole, and a singular one at that. Take a look at these example compound subjects:

- gentleman and scholar
- spaghetti and marinara
- peanut butter and jelly
- sister and best friend

Compound subjects that represent a singular unit take a singular verb:

> Peanut butter and jelly ranks number one on my list of sandwich favorites.

> Spaghetti and marinara tastes great and is easy to prepare.

Each and *Every* in Compound Form

What happens when the words *each* and *every* create a compound subject? These words are singular in concept; therefore, when they introduce a compound subject, we count that subject as a singular concept.

Let's look at a couple of examples:

> <u>Each clap and whistle drives</u> the cast to bow once more.

> <u>Every minute and second counts</u> in the race.

Plural Forms with a Singular Concept

Some words end in *s* and have no plural form. We treat them as singulars.

Here are a few examples:

- mathematics
- molasses
- news

They take a singular verb form:

> Often, local television <u>news presents</u> a local bias.

> <u>Mathematics involves</u> the study of systems and numbers.

When you're not sure about words like these, your dictionary is an easy resource to turn to. It will tell you whether the word takes a singular or plural verb form. Because words may have several meanings, you may have to scan through the definitions to find the relevant one.

Plural Forms with a Plural Concept

This next list has examples of yet another group of words. These words end in *s*, and we treat them as plurals:

- handcuffs
- pants
- scissors
- tights
- tweezers

Notice that these are words for things that are one piece made up of two parts. We partner them with a plural verb form:

> My <u>scissors are</u> often in the wrong place.
>
> Usually, <u>handcuffs do work</u> as a sufficient restraint.

You're on your way to becoming a master of subject-verb agreement!

Lesson 2: Singular or Plural?

Next we're going to look at nouns and pronouns that are a little out of the ordinary. To ensure agreement, we have to understand if they're singular or plural. We'll examine:

- plurals that go both ways
- singulars joined by *or* or by correlatives
- singulars and plurals joined by *or* or by correlatives

Plural Forms That Go Both Ways

Beyond the collectives you looked at last lesson, there are other words that can be singular or plural depending on context. Here are a few examples:

- ethics
- politics
- semantics
- statistics

We have to make case-by-case decisions about these words. It helps to consider them in sentences:

> Singular: <u>Ethics is</u> a branch of philosophy.
>
> (In this sentence, *ethics* is a subject area, like English or math.)
>
> Plural: The leaders' <u>ethics are</u> seen as controversial, some considered moral, some immoral.
>
> (In this subject, *ethics* is plural noun, like *principles*.)

Singulars Joined by *Or* or by Correlative Conjunctions

Different kinds of conjunctions have different effects on the relationship between subjects and verbs.

Or

Though the conjunction *and* works like a plus sign and creates a compound subject that takes a plural verb form, something different happens when we replace *and* with *or*. If we're joining two singulars, the verb becomes singular. Take a look:

> <u>Fred and Tom are</u> the names of my goldfish.
>
> Sometimes I can't remember if <u>Frank or Francis is</u> the name of my grandson's goldfish.

Correlative Conjunctions

Correlative conjunctions correlate or match two parts of a sentence to each other. These conjunctions are word pairs that join elements of equal weight, such as subject to subject:

- either/or
- neither/nor
- not only/but also
- not/but

Singulars Joined by Correlative Conjunctions

When joining singulars with correlatives, the subject-verb relationship follows the same rule as it does when we use the word *or*. Here's an example:

> Neither Fred nor Tom is a suitable name for my goldfish.

Singulars and Plurals Joined by Correlative Conjunctions

Something different happens when we join a singular and a plural subject with this group of conjunctions. The subject closest to the verb directs the verb:

> Singular: Not only her three silver knives but also her one gold fork needs polishing.

> Plural: Either his one gold fork or his three silver knives need polishing.

Lesson 3: Between Subject and Verb

You've looked at a variety of subject types and seen how to ensure they agree with their verbs. Now we're going to look at sentences that have words coming between subject and verb and at sentences with verbs that come before their subjects.

Phew!

In cases like these, your goal is to work around, dodge through, or jump over the sentence structure to make sure the subject and verb are in agreement.

Three types of word groups frequently appear between subject and verb:

- prepositional phrases
- clauses
- parenthetical phrases

And these words can indicate a sentence with a verb before its subject:

- here
- there
- it

Prepositional Phrases

To ensure agreement, we're going to be on the alert for prepositional phrases that come between subjects and verbs. It's easy to mistake the object of a preposition for the sentence subject.

(Reminder: A sentence subject can't be in a prepositional phrase.)

Example prepositional phrase:

> One <u>of the cafeteria diners</u> was disappointed that the establishment ran out of sweet potato fries.

We can break down the sentence this way:

> subject = one
>
> verb = was disappointed
>
> prepositional phrase = of the cafeteria diners

The noun *diners* is the object of the preposition *of*. Because the noun is adjacent to the verb, it might appear to be the sentence subject. But it's not.

To find your subject and verb, all you have to do is temporarily eliminate the intervening prepositional phrase.

Let's spot the subject, verb, and prepositional phrase in the next sentence and figure out why the subject and verb aren't in agreement:

> Splashes of cold water wakes up a sleepy person.

We can break it down like this:

> subject = splashes
>
> verb = wakes
>
> prepositional phrase = of water

In this case, the subject and verb don't agree. Instead, the verb is mistakenly agreeing with *water*, the object of the preposition *of*. If we change the verb from *wakes* to *wake*, then it will agree with the subject, *splashes*:

> <u>Splashes</u> of cold water <u>wake</u> up a sleepy person.

Clauses

A clause is a group of words that includes a subject and a predicate and may be dependent or independent. The previous sentence includes an example of a dependent clause: *that includes a subject and a predicate and may be dependent or independent.*

Dependent clauses often come between subject and verb. To ensure subject-verb agreement, you can use the elimination strategy again.

Here's a sentence with a dependent clause intervening between subject and verb:

> The cafeteria customer <u>who takes the last sugar packet</u> feels fortunate.

Let's remove the clause to get a better look at the subject and verb:

> The cafeteria <u>customer feels</u> fortunate.

Now we can clearly see that the word *customer* agrees with its verb, *feels.*

Parenthetical Phrases

Parenthetical phrases can also intervene between subject and verb. A parenthetical phrase provides extra information that the sentence can do without. These phrases are asides that may add detail, color, or flair, but they aren't essential to the sentence structure or meaning.

The following words are often cues that a parenthetical follows:

- as well as
- in addition to
- like
- rather than
- together with
- with

Typically, we set off a parenthetical phrase with commas on both ends. (You'll learn more about this punctuation strategy in an upcoming chapter.) The commas can help you spot and then eliminate the parenthetical phrase to ensure subject-verb agreement.

> At this cafeteria, the <u>spaghetti</u>, as well as the braised brussels sprouts, <u>is</u> not as good as your spaghetti or brussels sprouts.

> At this cafeteria, the <u>spaghetti is</u> not as good as your spaghetti or brussels sprouts.

Subject and verb agree!

Lesson 4: Here, There, and It

Here and There

We often kick off a sentence with the word *here* or *there*:

> Here are my missing gloves!

> There's your lost sock, in the drawer.

Because of the word order, *here* and *there* seem as if they're the subjects in the sentences above. In Chapter 4, we discussed the idea that they can't be sentence subjects. Now you can take that idea to make sure your subjects and verbs are in agreement.

You can change the word order to more clearly see if your subjects and verbs agree:

My missing <u>gloves are</u> here.

Your lost <u>sock is</u> there, in the drawer.

The words *gloves* and *sock* are the subjects of their respective sentences, and their verbs must agree with them.

What about It?

Unlike *here* and *there*, *it* does work as a sentence subject and takes a singular verb:

<u>It is</u> the only time of the day for napping.

Sometimes we encounter the singular subject *it* with a plural complement:

<u>It is</u> the <u>clocks</u> that you hear chiming.

This is grammatically awkward. You can easily solve the problem with some minor rewriting:

You hear the clocks chiming.

Those are clocks you hear chiming.

Lesson 5: Agreeable Pronouns

In this lesson, we're going to see how to make sure pronouns agree with their verbs and with their antecedents. In many cases, agreement comes naturally. We'll look at those and at cases that present questions.

Pronoun-Verb Agreement

Pronouns working as subjects must agree with their verbs in number. We'll go over some rules about pronoun number to ensure agreement.

Singular Pronouns

The following pronouns take a singular verb:

- anybody, anyone, anything
- everybody, everyone, everything
- no one, nobody, nothing
- somebody, someone, something
- each, either, neither, one

Examples:

> <u>Everybody is</u> a student.

> <u>Each wants</u> to have a turn!

Plural Pronouns

The following pronouns take a plural verb:

- both
- few
- many
- several

Example:

> <u>Many are</u> full-time students, while <u>few work</u> and take classes.

Both Ways

The following pronouns can take a singular or plural verb, depending on context:

- all
- any
- more
- most
- some

Examples:

> <u>More is</u> better than less.
>
> <u>More are</u> arriving.

It helps to look at the pronouns in context to understand if they're singular or plural. If the antecedent is plural, the pronoun will be plural; if the antecedent is singular, the pronoun will be singular:

> Out of sixty cross-country <u>runners</u>, <u>most are</u> expected to complete the race.

> With so much <u>work</u> on my plate due tomorrow, <u>some is</u> the best I can accomplish.

If context doesn't make your choice crystal clear, you can try substituting logical words for the pronoun to determine if it should take a singular or plural verb:

> Out of sixty cross-country <u>runners, fifty-six are</u> expected to complete the race.

> With so much <u>work</u> on my plate due tomorrow, a <u>small portion is</u> the best I can accomplish.

Lesson 6: Pronoun-Antecedent Agreement

Remember all that work you did on pronouns in the previous chapter? It's going to pay off now!

Pronouns must agree with their antecedents in number. Personal pronouns must also agree in person, and singular personal pronouns must additionally agree in gender. Take a look at these examples:

> The <u>duck and the goose</u> take <u>their</u> afternoon siestas at the same time each day. (The plural pronoun *their* agrees with its plural antecedent, *duck and goose*.)

> The <u>female</u> of some species does not protect <u>her</u> eggs. (The singular personal pronoun *her* agrees in person, number, and gender with its antecedent, *female*.)

Collective Nouns

Pronouns that refer to collective nouns are singular or plural depending on the context of the sentence:

> The full <u>cast</u> takes <u>its</u> bow simultaneously at the end of the show. (Singular pronoun *its* refers to *cast* as a singular concept.)

> The <u>cast</u> stay at different hotels during <u>their</u> city tour. (Plural pronoun *their* refers to *cast* as a plural concept.)

Singular Antecedents Joined by *And*

Two singular antecedents joined by the conjunction *and* equal a plural:

> If you had <u>one left brown shoe and one right black shoe</u>, you could wear <u>them</u> together to make a fashion statement. (Plural pronoun *them* refers to its plural antecedent, *one left brown shoe and one right black shoe*.)

Singular Antecedents Joined by *Or* or by Correlatives

Singular antecedents joined by the word *or* equal a singular. The same holds true for singulars joined with a pair of correlative conjunctions, like *neither/nor*:

> If you found only <u>one sock or one mitten</u>, <u>it</u> wouldn't make a pair of socks or mittens.

(Singular pronoun *it* refers to its singular antecedent, *one sock or one mitten.*)

Neither one sock nor one mitten can transform itself into a pair. (Singular pronoun *itself* reflects its singular antecedent, *one sock nor one mitten.*)

Singular and Plurals Joined by the Word *Or* or by Correlatives

When *or* or a pair of correlative conjunctions join a singular antecedent with a plural antecedent, the pronoun agrees with the closest antecedent:

If you want to add a side order to your oatmeal, order either hash brown potatoes or one bagel because it won't cost much more. (Singular *it* agrees with *one bagel.*)

If you want to add a side order to your oatmeal, order one bagel or hash brown potatoes because they won't cost much more. (Plural t*hey* agrees with *hash brown potatoes.*)

These last two examples, though grammatical, may seem odd and fuzzy, leading to confusion (something we explore in Chapter 11). You have the option of working around these awkward constructions by rewriting. Here's one way to rewrite:

You won't have to pay much more if you add a side order of one bagel or hash brown potatoes to your oatmeal.

Demonstrative Pronouns

Remember the words *this*, *that*, *those*, and *these*? They all agree with their partner nouns. The words *this* and *that* are singular; and the words *those* and *these* are plural. Take a look at these words in sentences:

> Which <u>flavor</u> do you want to try, <u>this</u> or <u>that</u>?
> Which <u>flavors</u> do you want to try, <u>these</u> or <u>those</u>?

Relative Pronouns

Relative pronouns *that*, *what*, *which*, and *who* must relate to their antecedents and subsequently to their verbs:

> You are the only <u>farmer who chooses</u> to rise
> an hour later. (Relative pronoun *who* refers to
> *farmer* and agrees with singular verb *chooses*.)

> She is one of many <u>farmers who choose</u> to rise
> an hour later. (Relative pronoun *who* refers to
> *farmers* and agrees with plural verb *choose*.)

IN A NUTSHELL

Agreement requires analysis. Sometimes you'll be able to analyze a sentence in a split second and be confident you've located the words that need to agree and partnered them correctly.

Sometimes, particularly in complex sentence structures, you'll have to strategize and separate one part of a sentence from the rest to pinpoint exactly who or what is supposed to agree with what or whom.

Back at the cafeteria, if you sit down and then realize you wanted to use one of those biodegradable straws to drink from a juice box, that's okay. You can go back to the supply station.

Writers don't always get things right the first time around. After you write, the next step is analysis. Now you know what to look for as you reexamine your writing and head toward harmonious partnerships between your subjects and verbs and your pronouns and antecedents. If your work lacks agreement, you can fix it by editing.

While editing your writing, keep an eye out for any errors in agreement. You know how to fix them!

FAQs

Q: What about company names? Do they go with a singular or plural pronoun?

A: Company names are almost always considered singular and, therefore, partner with singular pronoun *it*:

> A-to-Z Cleanouts does exactly what it says
> it will do.

In contrast, the names for sports teams are considered plural, so we partner them with plural pronoun *they*:

> The Mets may get to the World Series again if they
> keep up their current winning streak.

Q: I'm so confused! Why do we put an s at the end of a verb that's supposed to agree with a third person singular subject?

A: We can trace this back to the roots of the English language! Third person singular verbs have evolved from Latin to Old English to the language we speak and write today.

Chapter 9 Quiz

Question 1:

Choose the right verb to fill in the blank:

"Neither the outfielders nor the pitcher _____ sunglasses."

    a. wear

    b. wears

Question 2

Decide if the subject and verb agree or disagree:

"The fork, knife, and spoon, which some people refer to as cutlery, is typically used during a meal."

    a. agree

    b. disagree

Question 3

Which is true of the pronoun *all*?

    a. It must agree with a singular verb form.

    b. It must agree with a plural verb from.

    c. It agrees with a singular or plural verb, depending on context.

Answer Key: Q1: b Q2: b Q3: c

CHAPTER 10

ALONG THE SAME LINES

(shifts in person, tense, and structure)

Introduction

Suppose that today after work, you decide to pick up fast food. You pull into the drive-through lane of Fast Fast Veggie Burger and Things (FFVB&T), whose motto is "We fix 'em how you like 'em." It's your go-to place. You count on it.

You ask for two veggie burgers with ketchup and pickles, a large order of onion rings, a medium sparkling black raspberry juice, and a couple of extra ketchup packets.

Moments later, you pick up your food at the drive-through window. Your order costs $11.11, as it always does.

You hand the cashier a twenty-dollar bill, and while waiting for your change, you ask as you do every time, just to be sure, "The veggie burgers don't have any mustard on them, right?"

"Right!" the cashier replies.

When you get home and unwrap the first veggie burger, you discover that FFVB&T made some mistakes: One of your burgers is slathered in mustard! The second burger is okay, but the carton of onion rings is upside down, and your sparkling black raspberry juice is small, not medium. FFVB&T also neglected to include extra ketchup packets. Darn!

You'll eat your meal. But you're disappointed. You didn't get what you were expecting.

Just as there's a system for building a veggie burger sandwich and putting fast food into a bag, there's a system for building the text you write. As chef, you want to prepare the food according to what a customer wants. As writer, you want to stick with a system unless and until there's a need for change.

In this chapter, we're going to look at different types of inconsistencies and how to correct them: shifts in person, tense, and structure.

Recognizing and fixing these problems will give your writing balance and clarity. You'll be able to give your readers what they expect!

Lesson 1: Shifts in Person and Tense

Before we jump in, here's a quick refresher on a few things you learned in previous lessons:

- When you write, you narrate in first, second, or third person.
- When you choose person, you simultaneously choose number—singular or plural—because number is part of person.
- When you narrate, you also decide to write in the past, present, or future tense.

You work in a *foundation person* and a *foundation tense*. Your goal is to remain consistent unless there's a good reason to make a change. A *shift* is a change. Some shifts are grammatical; others aren't.

Shifts in Person

If you're giving a speech in front of an audience, you'll naturally and appropriately make shifts in person and number. When you talk about your personal experience or knowledge, you use the first person singular: *I*. When you make a direct address to the audience, you use the second person plural: *you*. When you include the audience and yourself, you use first person plural: *we*.

The same applies to writing. Context dictates appropriate shifts.

Here's a sentence example with appropriate shifts in person:

> I like my fruit slightly ripe, <u>you</u> like your fruit very ripe, and if <u>we</u> ever shop for produce together, <u>we</u> will compromise and buy moderately ripe fruit.

Those examples are fine.

But in many cases, shifts in person are ungrammatical. Here's an example:

> Suppose <u>I</u> begin writing a paper in first person and next thing <u>you</u> know it's in second person. As a writer, <u>you</u> are losing sight of who's responsible for my words. Typically this happens when <u>one</u> is in unfamiliar or sensitive territory and is seeking a connection to the reading audience. When <u>you</u> shift from *I* to *you*, <u>we</u> lose our conviction. <u>They</u> are shifting credit—or blame—for my thoughts away from <u>yourself</u>.

Oh, boy! We're not sure whose thoughts are being expressed. Meaning is muddled, and shifts in person can also lead to pronoun-antecedent agreement problems.

Now that you've seen an example of what can go wrong, you're equipped to make person consistent in your writing. The rule is simple: Stick with the foundation person unless there's a reason to change.

Shifts in Tense

Just as you establish a foundation person, you also establish a foundation verb tense. Often, one or more shifts are necessary and appropriate in order to explain events that take place over a period of time.

The following paragraph uses three tenses. As you read, consider whether or not the shifts seem right:

> Fast Fast Veggie Burger and Things is probably still my favorite fast-food restaurant in spite of some mixed-up orders. Up until a week ago, I went there at least once a week. It was cheap, quick, and good. Last week, however, the place raised its prices and had a staff turnover. From now on, I think I will go only once or twice a month.

The shifts in tense are fine! The foundation is present tense. Events that occurred in the past are expressed in past tense. As future actions are considered, the tense shifts to the future. The text establishes a timeline in a logical manner.

Inappropriate shifts occur when there's no reason to make a change from the foundation tense. Here's an example:

> Mr. Gray <u>taught</u> us about shifts, and he <u>talks</u> so
> quietly that the class <u>lost</u> focus.

Oops! The shift from past to present is ungrammatical.

Though we tend to accept this kind of shift when people are speaking casually, it can still be confusing. We don't know for sure what's happening when. In writing, shifts in tense are even more noticeable and more confusing.

Lesson 2: Parallel Structure

Parallel structure, also called *parallelism*, is a system for putting items in a series into a consistent form. The serial items may range from words to phrases to lengthy clauses to sentences.

We use parallel structure for sentence parts that are equal in importance. Parallelism creates balance by keeping these parts in the same form, and it helps readers understand meaning.

First, we'll look at items in a series within a single sentence or list.

One little word is missing from the example sentence below. Without it, the sentence has a problem. You might like to read the sentence aloud to discover if you can hear the omission:

> Dietitians advise people <u>to drink</u> several glasses
> of water, <u>to eat</u> a balanced breakfast, <u>to moderate</u>
> caffeine intake, and <u>limit</u> fats and sugars.

Did you catch the lack of parallel construction? The sentence is only one small beat off its established pattern.

If you didn't find it, you can spot it when the serial elements are in list form:

- to drink several glasses of water
- to eat a balanced breakfast
- to moderate caffeine intake
- limit fats and sugars

All but the last item begin with the word *to*. That little word puts the verbs into infinitive form. To be parallel, the last item should be in the same form as the preceding ones:

- to limit fats and sugars

In the following example, it's possible to take a different approach and still achieve parallelism:

> Dietitians advise people <u>to drink</u> several glasses of water, <u>eat</u> a balanced breakfast, <u>moderate</u> caffeine intake, and <u>limit</u> fats and sugars.

Now, only the first item begins with the word *to*—to drink several glasses of water—and *to* is implied for the others. That's allowable, and it's often preferable to avoid unnecessary repetition.

Let's play with the sentence. Can you find the missing word that accounts for lack of parallel structure in the sentence below?

> Dietitians say, "You <u>should drink</u> several glasses of water, <u>should eat</u> a balanced breakfast, <u>moderate</u> caffeine intake, and <u>should limit</u> fats and sugars."

Repetition of the word *should* is creating extra emphasis. Something is wrong because this word is missing from one serial element—moderate caffeine intake.

To be parallel, only the first item should have the word *should*, or all items should have the word *should*.

Parallel structure is especially helpful in creating lists and outlines, but we can apply the concept to writing in general.

If you were the manager at FFVB&T, you might have an instructional reference poster for new employees who are learning how to put together a veggie burger sandwich.

. . . .

How to Put Together a Veggie Burger Sandwich

1. Open bun.

2. Place cooked patty on bottom half of bun.

3. Squeeze one teaspoon of ketchup in center of patty.

4. Arrange chopped pickles in circular pattern on top of ketchup.

5. Placing bun on top of finished sandwich.

. . . .

Did you notice that last list item isn't parallel to the others? That last instruction sounds unfinished. What's supposed to happen next?

Here's a simple change that solves the problem:

> 5. Place bun top on top of finished sandwich.

Suppose you were required to create an outline for an upcoming essay, letter, or business report. Making your outline items parallel could help you determine what should be included in your writing and could help you present your ideas in a clear and balanced way.

There are almost always different ways to approach the goal of parallelism.

Let's bake a cake to demonstrate!

Below are some phrases related to the process of baking a birthday cake:

- preheating the oven
- grease the pan
- prepare in advance
- to shop for supplies
- ensured freshness
- selection of candles
- decorations
- number of servings

If you were to turn these phrases, currently presented in a variety of forms, into a list or outline, in chronological order, how might you go about it?

We have possibilities.

Put each item in the form of a directive:

· ·

How to Bake a Cake

1. Prepare in advance.

2. Determine number of servings.

3. Shop for supplies shortly before preparation.

4. Select candles and decorations.

5. Take out all ingredients.

6. Preheat the oven.

7. Grease the pan.

8. Follow the recipe.

· ·

Or you might convert each verb into a gerund and create a complete sentence:

· ·

Cake Baking From Prep to Completion

- Determining the number of required servings will help you adjust recipe amounts.

- Shopping for supplies shortly before preparation will ensure freshness.

- Selecting candles and decorations now will save you a return trip to the store.

- Taking out all of the ingredients will keep you organized.

- Preheating the oven will save you time.

- Greasing the pan will prevent sticking.

- Following the recipe will result in a great cake.

· ·

Voila! You've made a cake.

And you've learned that using parallel structure improves your writing.

Lesson 3: More Structural Shifts

Have you ever gleaned the meaning of a sentence while at the same time sensing something was not quite right? A sentence that seems illogical or somehow wrong could be a *mixed construction* or an *incomplete comparison*.

These structural problems result when sentence parts don't successfully work together.

Sticking to a few rules puts you in charge and paves the way to avoiding and fixing shifts.

Mixed Constructions

A mixed construction occurs when two parts of a sentence—subject and predicate or subject and complement—don't go together. That means the two parts don't logically connect.

To fix these mixed constructions, we need to change or add some words.

Illogical Subjects

We'll begin with subjects that are illogical because they're where they don't belong:

- inside prepositional phrases
- inside clauses beginning with subordinating conjunctions

Here's a prepositional phrase as an illogical subject:

> <u>In the quiet, early morning hours</u> helps students concentrate while studying for final exams.

If you try to locate the subject of the sentence, you'll probably have trouble.

That's because the subject is in the prepositional phrase: In the quiet, early morning hours.

But you know when it comes to good grammar, that's not allowed. To make a logical subject, you need to remove it from the prepositional phrase.

You probably understand that the sentence means the following:

> The quiet, early morning hours can be an ideal time for students to concentrate while studying for final exams.

Now the sentence has a real and logical subject.

(Note that when you eliminate the preposition, you may also have to make small adjustments to the rest of the sentence.)

Though some dependent clauses can function as sentence subjects, others can't. Here are a couple of examples of clauses that are illogical subjects:

> <u>Although I wanted to go</u> wasn't enough of a reason.

> <u>Because the bus ride was so long, bumpy, and hot</u> made students feel sick upon returning to the classroom.

Are you able to find the sentence subjects? Each is buried within the dependent clause.

Let's free each subject from its clause and rewrite the sentences.

Logical possibilities are:

> I wanted to go, but that wasn't enough of a reason.

> The long, bumpy, hot bus ride made students feel sick upon returning to the classroom.

Illogical Predicates

Likewise, the predicate of a sentence can't be in a dependent clause.

Here's an example of an illogical predicate:

> The number of high school students who don't get enough sleep, which is on the rise due to earlier school start times.

What's the predicate of the sentence? You'll find the predicate within the dependent clause beginning with the word *which*. But the predicate of a sentence can't be in a dependent clause.

A sentence like this is easy to correct. All you have to do is free the predicate by removing the word that makes the clause dependent:

> The number of high school students who don't get enough sleep is on the rise due to earlier school start times.

Illogical Complements

A quick refresher: A complement follows a linking verb. Complements "equal" their subjects. Complements are nouns or adjectives.

Here's an example of an illogical complement:

> The health problems that result because young children are going to bed later and getting up earlier are <u>when pediatricians get motivated to issue guidelines for healthier sleep habits</u>.

What's wrong with this sentence? It tells us that the health problems are *when*. But *when* is an adverb, and an adverb can't be a complement.

You can use different approaches to correct this sentence. You could adjust the subject, adjust the complement, or rewrite the sentence.

Here's one suggestion:

> The health problems that result because young children are going to bed later and getting up earlier motivate pediatricians to issue guidelines for healthier sleep habits.

In this rewrite, we removed the linking verb *are* and the adverb *when* and replaced them with the action verb *motivate*. A little rewriting goes a long way!

Incomplete Comparisons

Complete comparisons must be grammatically parallel. Like a balanced seesaw, a complete comparison requires equally weighted elements on both ends.

An incomplete comparison results when something is missing from what should be parallel parts of a sentence:

> He appreciates fiction books more than most of his friends.

We have to wonder: What's being compared to what? The sentence could mean either of the following:

> He likes fiction books more than he likes most of his friends.

He likes fiction books more than most of his friends do.

The logical answer is that his appreciation of fiction books is being compared to his friends' appreciation of fiction books. Therefore, the sentence needs to make clear that *he* and *his friends* are parallel.

Faulty comparisons usually omit words or contain words that are in the wrong form. You can correct them by adding the necessary words or changing word forms.

IN A NUTSHELL

In this chapter, you learned about grammar problems related to inconsistency. These problems can interfere with meaning.

You can achieve consistency in person, tense, and structure by following some basic rules of grammar:

Establish foundation person and tense.

Shift only when necessary.

Build even and complete structures.

Consistent writing is different from dull writing. If every sentence followed the same pattern, and if every paragraph were structurally formatted in exactly the same way as the one before it and the one after it, your readers would lose focus because of an overabundance of familiarity. In other words, they'd get bored.

Consistency is compatible with variety.

Choosing your foundation person and tense, creating parallelism in your serial elements, and keeping your sentences structurally sound will allow you to word complex ideas in a way that offers your readers the best possible opportunity to understand exactly what you want to express.

Natural and necessary grammatical shifts will be a part of your writing.

You're the chef! Build your text with the basic, necessary ingredients. Then, top with pickles if that's what the customer ordered. (And remember to place the onion rings upright in the bag.)

When you write, be on the lookout for any shifts in person, tense, or structure.

Q: Is it wrong to make a shift in mood?

A: Whenever possible, it's best to keep mood consistent in the same way it's best to keep person, tense, and structure consistent.

For example, if you're writing instructions in the imperative mood (giving orders), stick with the imperative. If you're writing in the indicative (making statements), stick with the indicative.

Here's an example that shifts from imperative to indicative:

> Unhook the safety belt to gain access to the device, and then you should press the lever to open it.

Here it is improved by maintaining consistency:

> Unhook the safety belt to gain access to the device, and then press the lever to open it.

Q: Why is dialogue written with the tags in past tense even if the story is written in another tense? Doesn't that create a shift in tense?

A: Though this is technically a shift in tense, it's not considered an error; it's a standard, accepted storytelling convention.

Dialogue tags like "he whispered" or "she said"—also called *attributions*—are conventionally written in the past tense, no matter the foundation tense of the story. However, some writers who use present tense elect to keep the tags in present tense too, and that's a valid choice.

Chapter 10 Quiz

Question 1

Decide if this sentence has a shift in person or tense or is okay:

"You should have an interest in the subject matter, or else one may not be motivated to do the work."

    a. shift in person

    b. shift in tense

    c. okay as is

Question 2

Decide if this sentence has a shift in person or tense or is okay:

"During most of the game, they were in the losing position, but when the last seconds of the final quarter arrived, they move into the winning position."

    a. shift in person

    b. shift in tense

    c. okay as is

Question 3

Decide if the comparison is complete or incomplete:

"She likes winter weather more than her brother."

    a. complete

    b. incomplete

Answer Key: Q1:a Q2:b Q3:b

CHAPTER 11:

SAY WHAT YOU MEAN

(clarity, concision, diction, and logic)

Introduction

> **KEYWORDS:**
>
> ◊ syntax ◊ wordiness
>
> ◊ misplaced modifiers ◊ concision
>
> ◊ dangling modifiers ◊ diction
>
> ◊ ambiguous modifiers ◊ logic
>
> ◊ faulty reference

Have you ever been involved in a simple misunderstanding that blew up into a heated argument because somebody misconstrued your words or you misinterpreted theirs?

Our words aren't always crystal clear.

In this chapter, we'll continue to explore ways to make your writing clear and accurate.

Your work in recognizing and fixing shifts in person, tense, and structure has helped prepare you for this chapter. Here you'll equip yourself with more ways to produce text that's structurally sound and logical. Good grammar doesn't, however, always correlate to good sense. So together, we'll also make sure that you say what you mean and mean what you say. And we'll work on getting rid of any extra junk that stands in the way.

In our social world, we follow many types of etiquette. There's an etiquette for just about any ritual you can imagine: how to set a table, how to use the lap lanes in a swimming pool, how to board an elevator full of people, or how to stand in line for a movie.

If you choose to follow etiquette for setting a table, chances are you'll have a napkin on hand when you need one. In many cultures, you'll have a fork for pasta primavera and a spoon for coconut milk pudding. The fork and spoon will be in the right place too. You could almost reach for them without looking.

Etiquette and grammar have some things in common. Both provide a code of convention. Thoughtfully structured sentences that say what the writer intended follow a grammar etiquette.

In this chapter, we'll concentrate on the order of words and phrases as they affect meaning. We'll also look at what you might have left out, what you need to include, what you should leave out, and what's appropriate in the environment of your sentences.

That's a lot of *whats*. But they're worth looking at because you have a triple goal: to be clear, to be concise, and to say what you mean.

Lesson 1: Syntax and Modifiers

Just as there's a system for placing forks, knives, and spoons at a table, there's a system for placing words in a sentence. *Word order* is called *syntax*, and syntax affects meaning. In this chapter, we'll focus on the placement of modifiers and the effect of placement on meaning.

A modifier can be a single word, like an adjective or adverb, or it can be a group of words, like a phrase or clause. Likewise, a modifier can describe a single word, like a verb, or a group of words, like a phrase.

Poor syntax can lead to sentences that are funny or ridiculous at best and ambiguous or misstated at worst. Modifiers are some of the chief culprits in word-order problems.

We'll look at:

- misplaced modifiers
- dangling modifiers
- ambiguous modifiers

Syntax and Meaning

To show the effect of syntax on meaning, we'll start with two sentences that are grammatically and logically sound. The sentences contain identical words, but different word order:

> We looked out to sea <u>hopefully, praying</u> that the lost swimmer would reappear.
>
> We looked out to sea, <u>praying hopefully</u> that the lost swimmer would reappear.

Meaning can change according to the placement of one word. In the first sentence, the adverb *hopefully* is working with the verb *looked*. We are, therefore, looking out to sea with hope. In the second sentence, *hopefully* is working with the verb *praying*. Now we're praying with hope. Both of these sentences work successfully even though their meanings are a little bit different.

Now let's look at some other sentence examples to see what makes them confusing or wrong.

Misplaced Modifiers

Misplaced modifiers, as their name indicates, are in the wrong place. They end up describing the wrong thing:

> The kid was hungry and wanted to eat his peanut butter and jelly sandwich, so he skipped home <u>ravenously</u>.

At a glance, we understand what this sentence likely means:

> The kid skipped home because he was ravenous and wanted to eat his sandwich.

The sentence means to tell us that the kid was *ravenously hungry*, but it tells us that he *skipped ravenously*.

Let's change the word order to reflect intended meaning:

> The kid was <u>ravenously</u> hungry and wanted to eat his peanut butter and jelly sandwich, so he skipped home.

Syntax matters. It's best to place modifiers as close as possible to the word or words they're intended to describe.

Dangling Modifiers

Dangling modifiers are dangling because they have nothing to modify. The thing they're intended to describe is missing from the sentence. It's easy, therefore, for a reader to relate the modifier to the next closest word. This can lead to all kinds of problems, including confusion, humor, or nonsense.

Here's a classic dangling modifier:

> After wandering around lost for hours on
> the hiking path, our backpacks felt heavier
> and heavier.

As it stands, the modifying phrase "after wandering around lost for hours on the hiking path" is modifying the sentence subject *backpacks*. Logic tells us, though, that the backpacks aren't wandering around lost.

You can fix the dangling modifier by rewriting the sentence to include what was missing.

Here are two suggestions:

> After wandering around lost for hours on the
> hiking path, we felt as if our backpacks were
> getting heavier and heavier.

> After we'd been wandering around lost for hours
> on the hiking path, our backpacks felt heavier
> and heavier.

Ambiguous Modifiers

Sometimes, a modifier simultaneously describes two things in a sentence. This act of double duty results in ambiguity.

Here's an example of an *ambiguous modifier*:

> Film reviewers who write powerfully sway the
> movie-going audience.

The word *powerfully* is a modifier that could be describing the verb *write*, or the verb *sway*.

First you have to decide what the modifier is modifying. Then, to end the ambiguity, you'll likely have to revise the sentence.

Here are two possibilities:

> Film reviewers who write with power sway the audience.

> Film reviewers can significantly sway the audience.

Lesson 2: Faulty Reference

Faulty reference occurs when a pronoun doesn't have a clear antecedent or lacks one altogether. We'll look at two types of faulty reference:

- ambiguous pronouns
- dangling pronouns

Ambiguous Pronouns

Pronouns can be ambiguous just as modifiers can. An *ambiguous pronoun* has two or more possible antecedents:

> The girl asked her mother if <u>she</u> would be home in time to watch their favorite show.

> > We're not sure if the pronoun *she* refers to *girl* or to *mother*.

Now let's work on fixing the problem. There's almost always more than one way to do that. The first step is to analyze the sentence.

Step One: Determine what the sentence is supposed to mean. If the word *mother* is the antecedent, the sentence means:

> The girl asked if her mother would be home in time to watch their favorite show.

If the word *girl* is the antecedent, the sentence means:

> The girl wanted to know if she, herself, would be home in time to watch their favorite show.

Step Two: Revise the sentence to make the antecedent clear. Let's suppose that the word *mother* is the antecedent. Take a look:

> The girl asked her mother if her mother would be home in time to watch their favorite show.

This solution, while clarifying the antecedent, is tedious with its repetitive phrases. Rewriting with a direct quotation is one way to eliminate that problem:

> The girl asked her mother, "Will you be home in time to watch our favorite show?"

If the word *girl* is the antecedent, the sentence could read as follows:

> The girl asked her mother, "Will I be home in time to watch our favorite show?"

Here's another ambiguous pronoun:

> I asked for a short stack of gluten-free pancakes
> topped with blueberries, but got two plates with
> one cold pancake on each, with blueberries in a
> side dish, <u>which</u> is not my preference.

We're not sure if the relative pronoun clause, *which is not my preference*, refers to one, all, or any combination of the ways in which the pancakes and blueberries were served.

Here's a possible rewrite:

> I asked for a short stack of gluten-free pancakes
> topped with blueberries but got two plates with
> one cold pancake on each, with blueberries in a
> side dish. I wanted hot pancakes with blueberries
> on top—all on one plate.

You get to solve a puzzle when you fix ambiguous pronouns!

Dangling Pronouns

A *dangling pronoun* lacks an antecedent in the same way as a dangling modifier lacks something to describe:

> When he looked back on his education, he
> realized that he never took any courses in
> psychology, yet he still wished he could be one.

The pronoun *one* has no antecedent. Did he wish that he could be *courses in psychology*? That solution doesn't make sense.

It's easy to create this kind of faulty reference problem. We might have all the details worked out in our minds but not in our writing.

To fix a sentence with a missing antecedent, first determine what the missing antecedent should be. Then rewrite in order to supply it.

To establish the missing sentence element, we want to answer the question: What does he wish he could be? One logical answer is *psychologist*.

Here's a suggested rewrite:

> When he looked back on his education, he realized that he never took any courses in psychology, yet he still wished he could be a psychologist.

Lesson 3: Wordiness

In this lesson, we'll explore *wordiness* and how to get rid of it.

When we speak, we often toss in a lot of extra words that aren't essential to our meaning. When we listen, we tend to be tolerant of wordiness because intonations and facial expressions add interest. We're less likely to be patient when we read. Wordiness slows us down and detracts from what's important. *Concision* is the opposite of wordiness. Concise writing gets to the point and helps to make the point clear.

The use of superfluous phrases, extra adverbs, and needless constructions and clauses results in wordiness. Let's look at different types of word clutter and see how to alter or eliminate it.

Superfluous Phrases

Here's a list of common wordy phrases and concise alternatives:

Wordy	Concise
the reason is that	because
it is my opinion that	I think
in this day and age	today
in the event of	if
3 a.m. in the morning	3 a.m.
my sister, she	my sister
at this point in time	now

In most cases, the concise alternative is the better option. Wordiness does have its place in writing. For example, you could use it in naturalistic dialogue.

Extra Adverbs and Phrases with *Of*

Look for unnecessary adverbs such as *clearly, interestingly, obviously, really,* and *totally.*

Wordy:

> You're <u>totally</u> engrossed in the <u>subject of grammar</u>.

Better:

> You're engrossed in the <u>subject of grammar</u>.

Even better:

> You're engrossed in <u>grammar</u>.

Needless Constructions

When a sentence begins with the word *there* or *it*, followed with a form of *to be*, the construction can sometimes be eliminated.

Wordy:

> There is a situation involving a warehouse with failing refrigeration, resulting in spoiled food.

Better:

> A situation involving a warehouse with failing refrigeration is resulting in spoiled food.

Needless Clauses

Clauses that begin with the relative pronouns *which*, *that*, *who*, and *whom* can sometimes be eliminated.

Wordy:

> The kitchen sink salad that was served to us was smaller than expected based on its price.

Better:

> The kitchen sink salad served to us was smaller than expected based on its price.

When looking to eliminate needless phrases and clauses, you don't want to sacrifice meaning for concision. If the phrase or clause is necessary to express what you want, or to add a desired emphasis, leave it.

Compare these two sentences:

The girl, <u>who was standing</u> on the corner when the accident occurred, was the only eyewitness.

The girl <u>standing</u> on the corner when the accident occurred was the only eyewitness.

In the first sentence, the relative pronoun clause adds a significant detail. The information stresses her position, whereas the second sentence stresses which girl she is.

Lesson 4: Diction and Logic

Some sentences can include all the necessary grammatical ingredients yet still be problematic because they use the wrong words or lack logic.

Diction

Diction is word choice. Informal writing calls for informal diction, and formal writing calls for formal diction. There are many shades of diction: academic, scientific, hifalutin, and poetic, to name a few.

Scientific writing, for example, belongs in text designed for scientists, not in a general information blog for laypeople. The wrong diction can be alienating to a reader.

When we're looking for word options to create variety and avoid repetition, a thesaurus can be a wonderful tool. This same tool can lead to word choice that's out of place, pompous, or plain old silly.

It's important to know how to use a word within the context of your writing. When you work with a thesaurus and find new words to replace ones you're accustomed to using, it's easy to select words that aren't a good fit.

Appropriate diction can also help with concision. Compare the sentences in each pair:

> **Pair 1**
>
> > The girl was <u>felicitous upon receiving</u> her allowance.
> >
> > The girl was <u>happy to get</u> her allowance.
>
> **Pair 2**
>
> > <u>I desire the opportunity to proffer</u> my prize azaleas at the <u>floral convention</u>.
> >
> > <u>I would like to present</u> my prize azaleas at the <u>flower show</u>.

Logic

Some sentences don't make sense even if all the grammatical elements are in place.

Consider this sentence:

> My goal for the summer is to try and put an end to people who do experiments on animals when they could be using a computer.

That sentence sounds threatening! Its literal meaning is very different from its intended meaning.

It says:

> My goal for the summer is to kill people who
> prefer doing experiments on animals rather than
> spending their time working on computers.

I'm pretty sure this literal meaning doesn't match
the intention.

Here's a possible rewrite:

> My goal for the summer is to try and put an end
> to vivisection when researchers instead could be
> using a computer to conduct their studies.

Being aware of diction and logic can work wonders when you
edit your writing. Before creating a final draft, try reading your
work and asking:

> Does the language fit the subject matter and the
> reading audience?
>
> Does it make good, plain sense?

A yes to both means you're on target. A no to one or both
questions means you have some editing to do.

IN A NUTSHELL

Restaurants specializing in greasy finger foods have a good reason to provide extra napkins and packaged hand wipes. This service convention makes eating the meal more relaxed... and neater!

Grammar conventions help us clarify our meaning and make it easier for us to express ourselves.

You're now equipped to eliminate misinterpretations that occur from fuzzy writing, excessive verbiage, and accidental nonsense.

In this chapter, you've applied your knowledge of modifiers, clauses, pronouns, and antecedents. You've considered how they work both structurally and contextually.

You've also explored the concepts of wordiness, word choice, and logic. Understanding these concepts will help you remove words that detract from your meaning. You can be concise and say what you mean.

Writing rarely turns out completely clear, concise, and logical the first time a writer puts words on the page or screen. That's what editing is for! When you edit, you refine your writing. When you dish out food, you can use a sponge to wipe up the soup that sloshes over the side of your bowl. Editing is the writer's sponge.

FAQs

Q: What about euphemisms? Are they considered wordy?

A: People use euphemisms with the intention of being polite, delicate, or politically correct. Euphemisms are typically wordier than their straightforward alternatives.

Compare two expressions:

> He passed to the other side.

> He died.

Consider your audience, and avoid euphemisms when you can, but not at the expense of diplomacy and sensitivity.

Q: If I use a thesaurus to find new words to say what I mean, how can I evaluate diction?

A: It's not easy to figure out the level of diction when you're unfamiliar with a word. Words have denotative and connotative meanings. Not all dictionaries offer enough information for you to make appropriate choices. A good dictionary is an invaluable resource. A thorough dictionary will provide usage notes that will help you understand how to use words in context.

One of the best ways to learn about words is to note how they're used as you come across them while reading.

Chapter 11 Quiz

Question 1

Name the grammar problem in the following sentence:

"I am inflamed to start reading my new book!"

    a. diction

    b. pronoun reference

    c. wordiness

Question 2

Decide if this sentence has a dangling modifier or is okay:

"While out with our baskets picking blueberries, some strawberries got in the mix."

    a. dangling modifier

    b. okay as is

Question 3

Name the grammar problem in this sentence:

"Although she spent nearly a decade studying ornithology at the esteemed Society for the Preservation of Bird Species, she never wished to become one professionally."

    a. modifier problem

    b. diction

    c. logic

Answer Key: Q1:a Q2:a Q3:c

HOW TO BEGIN AND WHY STOP AT A PERIOD?

(capitalization and punctuation)

Introduction

In this chapter, we'll cover the basic rules for capitalization and punctuation. You'll also learn some editing strategies.

When you're in line to pay for something, and it's time to put your items on the conveyor belt, do you reach for one of those bars to separate your items from those of the shoppers in front and in back of you? Or do you leave it up to the cashier to ask if something is yours?

In written language, there's no cashier. We have to rely on capitalization and punctuation to provide the signs to tell us when to start, pause, stop, and start again. Without these guideposts, language gets jumbled.

Following the basic rules of capitalization and punctuation is a way of fine-tuning your work to keep it organized and clear for your readers. You're the supervisor of your own writing. You're in charge of the conveyor belt of words and sentences.

KEYWORDS:

◇ capitalization

◇ punctuation

◇ end punctuation

◇ internal punctuation

◇ editing

Lesson 1: Capitalization

Yes, this part of grammar is all about rules. The good news is that most of the rules make sense. And it feels so good to know what to do and get things right!

If you're worried about how you'll remember all these rules, well, you don't need to worry. You can always come back to this book to look up what you've forgotten.

A capital letter is the first guidepost we see. It means: Here's the beginning of a sentence. We also use capital letters for many other purposes. In this lesson, we'll look at the *capitalization* rules for:

- first word in a sentence
- first person singular pronoun *I*
- names, initials, titles of people, and familial titles
- days, months, and holidays
- particular places
- religions, nationalities, languages, races, and cultures
- salutations and sign-offs
- titles of written works and major events
- first word of a direct quotation
- companies and organizations

Occasionally, I'll mention when not to capitalize.

✍ Tip

The instruction to capitalize refers to the first letter of a word, not the entire word.

Rule: Capitalize the first word of a sentence.

> Example:
>
> Who wants to go out for ice cream?

Rule: Capitalize the first-person singular pronoun *I*, wherever it appears.

> Examples:
>
> I want to!
>
> Believe me, I want to.

Rule: Capitalize names, initials, titles of people, and familial titles.

> Examples:
>
> Do you want to go out for ice cream, Ed?
>
> Do you go by Ed Rymes or Ed C. Rymes?
>
> His professional name is Vice President Edward C. Rymes.
>
> At home, we call him Uncle Ed.
>
> I named my goldfish Ed after Uncle Ed.

Typically, when a title comes after a name, it's lowercase. For example, you would not capitalize the words *vice president* in this sentence: "Edward C. Rymes is the vice president of the company."

We also don't capitalize job functions and family relationships when we use them generically. For example, in this sentence, you would not capitalize the word *uncle*: "To me, he's just an uncle."

Rule: Capitalize days of the week, months, and holidays.

> Example:

> Did you start reading this book on a Wednesday in May or on Memorial Day?

Rule: Capitalize specific places and regions.

> Examples:

> You may not be able to float in your bathtub or on the Delaware River, but everybody can float on the Great Salt Lake in Utah.

> Does your family come from the Southwest?

We don't capitalize directions. For instance, we wouldn't capitalize the word *south* in this sentence: "Let's drive south and see where the road takes us." In that example, the word *south* is a general direction, not a specific place.

The following are types of specific places that should be capitalized, with an example for each:

- bodies of water—the Dead Sea
- buildings—the Empire State Building
- streets—Main Street
- countries—Senegal
- cities—Seoul
- monuments—the Great Pyramid of Giza
- mountains—Mount Everest
- states—Montana
- continents—Antarctica
- planets—Mars

Lesson 2: More Capitalization Rules

The following rules give you the know-how to handle lots of everyday questions about what, exactly, should be capitalized.

Rule: Capitalize the name for religions, nationalities, languages, races, and cultures.

> Example:
>
> Though there is a large Puerto Rican community in New York City and there are many Cuban Americans in Miami, Spanish is but one of the many languages spoken in both cities.

Rule: Capitalize the first word of a salutation.

> Examples:
>
> Dear students,
>
> Hello, friends.

Some style guides say to capitalize all nouns that follow a salutation—for example, you could use a capital *S* in *Students*: Dear Students. And you could use a capital *F* in *Friends*: Hello, Friends.

Rule: Capitalize the first word of a sign-off.

> Examples:
>
> Very truly yours,
>
> Cordially,
>
> Your friend,

Rule: Capitalize titles of written works and major events.

Example:

The Diary of a Young Girl was written during World War II.

Typically, small words such as articles, conjunctions, and prepositions—*a, an, the, and, or, for, in, to*—are lowercase unless they begin the title. Do capitalize the beginning of a title.

✍ **Tip** _____

It's good practice to follow the capitalization that has already been established in a published work. Some authors choose to capitalize every word (or none).

_____

Rule: Capitalize the first word of quoted speech.

Example:

Teachers often ask, "What do you want to learn?"

Rule: Capitalize the names of companies and organizations.

Example:

If you want to stay current on potato news in England, the British Potato Council may be your best source.

If the company or organization begins with a lowercase letter, as in the case of *eBay Inc.*, don't capitalize the first letter. But if it begins a sentence, some style guides say to capitalize. You can reword to work around this.

Following already established capitalization isn't always easy. You'll find, for example, that within one single web page, a company may present the capitalization of its own name in two or more ways. Whatever you settle on, it's good to be consistent.

Lesson 3: End Punctuation

In this lesson, we'll cover basic punctuation rules for:

- the period .
- the question mark ?
- the exclamation point !

These three punctuation marks are *end punctuation*. Each creates what we call a *full stop*.

The term *full stop* makes sense when you connect it to the role of these punctuation marks. They make a statement: Halt and take a breath before continuing.

Let's get to the rules!

Rule: Use a period to end a sentence that makes a statement or issues a command.

>   Example:

>   Grammar is fun.

Tip

After a period, we use one space. The same is true after any end punctuation and after a colon.

This may seem odd if you were taught to use two spaces. But one space is today's norm.

Using one space consistently may seem like a small thing, but it will improve the overall presentation of your writing.

Rule: Use a question mark to end a sentence that poses a question.

Example:

Do you think grammar is fun?

Rule: Use an exclamation point to indicate real excitement.

Example:

Grammar is my favorite subject!

Try to hold back if you find yourself tempted to use lots of exclamation points throughout your writing. They lose their effect. When you lightly sprinkle the exclamation point, it will be effective.

Punctuating Sentence Fragments

We punctuate deliberate sentence fragments the same way we punctuate complete sentences.

Rule: Use a period, exclamation point, or question mark at the end of words or phrases with the same emphasis as when it punctuates a complete sentence.

> Examples:
>
> Not what I meant.
>
> Great idea!
>
> Joining us tonight?

Punctuation marks play an important role in shaping our understanding of text. The significance of a single word or an entire sentence can shift due to the way it's punctuated. For example, consider the difference in how you would read the word *Tortillas* followed by a period versus a question mark versus an exclamation point:

> Tortillas.
>
> Tortillas?
>
> Tortillas!

More about the Period

Periods have two other important uses.
Rule: Use a period to punctuate an initial.

> Example:
>
> Rocket J. Squirrel and Bullwinkle J. Moose are the full names of Rocky and Bullwinkle.

But follow already established punctuation in proper names. We don't include the period in proper names that have established themselves without it.

Example:

FAO Schwarz

Rule: Use a period to mark an abbreviation.

Examples:

6:21 a.m.

101st St.

vs.

Lesson 4: Internal Punctuation

In this lesson, we'll look at *internal punctuation*.

These punctuation marks represent pauses of varying degrees at different points within a sentence:

- comma ,
- semicolon ;
- colon :

Each mark represents a *partial stop*, the written equivalent of the pauses we make when speaking.

Does that mean we place a comma every time we pause? Not exactly. It's good to back up what feels natural with some real rules.

You've already learned some uses of these three punctuation marks in Chapter 6, when we looked at ways to fix run-on sentences. But there's more.

Comma

Rule: Use a comma to separate coordinate adjectives. (These are adjectives of equal weight. If you could use the word *and* in place of the commas, and you could change the order of the adjectives, you're working with coordinate adjectives.)

> Examples:
>
> The soft, rumpled, comfy quilt provided evidence that someone had been sleeping in the bed.
>
> The rules for commas are not as dry, complex, ambiguous, contradictory, and endless as you may be suspecting.

In the second example above, the last comma (a.k.a. the *Oxford comma*) is discretionary. That means you can elect to use it or not. You'll encounter grammar guides that say you should omit the last comma in short serial items, and others that say it's required. If you choose to use the last comma, be consistent. In long serial items, it's a good idea to include it to help your reader.

We don't use the comma in this sentence:

> The old wooden chair could not support much weight.

In that example, *wooden chair* is considered an entity. No comma is needed, therefore, between the word *old* and the word *wooden*.

Rule: Use a comma to separate items in a series.

> Examples:
>
> Reduce, reuse, and recycle are often called the three Rs.

Do you love chips, popcorn, nuts, and pretzels
mixed together?

Rule: Use a comma before coordinating conjunctions that join
two independent clauses. (See Chapter 6, Lesson 3.)

Example:

You'll be an expert on punctuation, and
then you'll become an expert proofreader of
your own work.

Rule: Use a comma after some introductory phrases.

Example:

After phrases that are lengthy and don't
flow smoothly into the body of the sentence,
use a comma.

Some sentences need a comma after a short introductory
phrase to prevent a misreading.

Examples:

After eating, the green frogs rest and
sun themselves.

In the forest, green frogs can
camouflage themselves.

In the next example, the comma isn't necessary:

At night the frogs are noisy.

Rule: Use a comma after a dependent clause that precedes an independent clause.

> Examples:
>
> After we looked for green frogs, blue sea urchins, purple flowers, and red snakes all day long, the black of night was a relief.
>
> If you're ever in my neighborhood, please knock on my door to say hello!

Rule: Place commas before and after things that could be removed without affecting the grammar and logic of a sentence: names in a direct address (calling someone by name), *yes* and *no*, nonessential material, interrupters, and appositives.

> Examples:
>
> Do you believe, Sally, that you can do it?
>
> Yes, you do believe you can do it.
>
> Do you believe, therefore, that you can do it?
>
> Sally, the girl made famous because her name appeared in reading primers during the 1950s, wished that she had been named something else.

In that last example, the material enclosed in commas is called an *appositive*. An appositive renames something previously named. Although it supplies extra information, the information is usually not essential to the sentence.

Rule: Place a comma before and after a state name in city/ state and month-day/year constructions.

Example:

My friend grew up in El Paso, Texas, but moved to Seattle, Washington, for a new job.

How do you feel about having been born on January 1, 2001, at 12:01 a.m.?

Semicolon

Rule: Use a semicolon to join two closely related independent clauses. The second clause may contain a conjunctive adverb or transitional phrase.

Examples:

You've learned to recognize independent clauses; therefore, the semicolon will be easy for you.

The ice cream began to melt; the sun was hot enough to liquefy a whole gallon.

The campers wanted to go for a swim; on the other hand, the counselors wanted to take a nap.

Rule: Use a semicolon to separate lengthy serial items that contain commas.

Example:

When Aunt Felicity asked you to do the shopping, she made a list that said: buy almond milk; organic broccoli, florets if possible; carrots, with or without tops; almond milk yogurt, any flavor, any brand; tomatoes, preferably ripe; and two loaves of bread, whole wheat or rye.

Colon

Rule: Use a colon to announce that more information will follow.

> Example:
>
> Mr. Gray wanted all his students to achieve something: the ability to use punctuation correctly.

The information that follows a colon is often a list, a quotation, or an explanation, but it may be a single word. For example, notice the single word at the end of this sentence:

> When you get to the end of this chapter, you'll want to practice editing for one particular area of grammar: punctuation.

 **Tip** _____

We often use colons to announce lists, and lists have their own style considerations for introducing and punctuating items. When you create a list, whatever style you choose, consistency is key.

_____

Lesson 5: More Punctuation Marks

In this lesson, we'll look at the rules for:

- apostrophe '
- parentheses ( )
- brackets [ ]
- ellipsis …

- hyphen -
- em dash ——
- slash /

Apostrophe

We use apostrophes to form contractions and possessives. You're already an apostrophe ace. (See Chapter 3.)

Parentheses and Dashes

We use parentheses and em dashes for similar purposes and sometimes interchangeably, but these two marks are subtly different from one another. They illustrate how punctuation can be both a stylistic and grammatical choice.

Both marks set off text that breaks the flow or adds information. We use parentheses in writing in much the same way you might put your hand up to your mouth and turn your head a bit when uttering a verbal aside. Dashes, on the other hand, are more like saying, "Oh, and be sure to pay attention to this."

> Examples:
>
> Most boat owners name their boats (a practice that may seem funny to those who don't have or

love boats), and it may come as no surprise to you that the most popular boat name is Obsession.

The only two days of the year when there are no professional sports games—and I'm talking about MLB, NBA, NHL, and NFL games—are the day before and the day after the Major League Baseball All-Star Game.

Some grammar guides say parentheses should offset text that is less important than the rest of the sentence, while dashes should offset text that requires special notice.

Ultimately, the concept of more or less important is subjective. Many writers simply like to use one mark more than the other.

Ellipsis

Rule: Use the ellipsis to indicate that you're leaving out a word or words.

Some style guides dictate that you should treat an ellipsis typographically as a word and, therefore, leave a space on either side of it. Eliminate the preceding space when the ellipsis begins a sentence. Some publications use an internal space between each of the points that make up the ellipsis, and some don't.

What does all this mean? It's another case of choose a style and stick with it for consistency.

Example:

The wisdom of this old nursery rhyme has yet to be validated: "An apple a day keeps the doctor

away... Three each day, seven days a week—
ruddy apple, ruddy cheek."

The ellipsis stands in for omitted words just as the apostrophe stands in for missing letters in a contraction. You'll see ellipses used in the middle of quoted material and at the end of a sentence. Occasionally they come at the beginning of a quotation.

✍ **Tip** _____

> Best practices in writing tell us not to let the ellipsis compromise the integrity of a quotation. If you have to use a partial quotation, evaluate it to be sure it reflects the meaning of the larger context.

_____

We can also use the ellipsis to represent a pause in thought, as in this sentence:
"Well... yes, let's do it!"

Brackets

Rule: Use brackets for editorial commenting.

We use brackets in quoted material to indicate a comment or inclusion of words by someone other than the quoted person. For example, a newspaper editor may add bracketed material to clarify direct and natural speech in a limited context.

Example:

Connors went on to comment, "Residents are already paying up to $50,000 in [municipal] taxes, a sure sign that there must be a compromise on the local front."

Rule: Use brackets for a parenthetical within parentheses.

Example:

Fortunately (and I say "fortunately" because too much punctuation can be difficult for any reader [of any level], if you know what I mean), we don't use brackets this way very often.

Hyphen

Rule: Use a hyphen to connect two or more words that can be considered a single unit.

Examples:

The sugar-sprinkled peanuts were the sweetest snack on the tray.

Forty-five people showed up for the party.

✍ **Tip** _____

Though you'll often hear the hyphen referred to as a dash and vice versa, they're not interchangeable. You can visually distinguish between them. The hyphen connects; the dash offsets.

Slash

Rule: Use a slash to indicate an either/or concept.

> Example:
>
> When the building was reconstructed, all restrooms were made coed, and each door was marked with a big sign that read "He/She/They."

Lesson 6: Quotation Marks

Quotation marks get their own lesson because there are lots of rules for using them; plus we need to know how to use them with other punctuation marks.

Rule: Use quotation marks to indicate someone's exact words.

> Example:
>
> My grandmother, maven of pithy sayings, loved these words: "Don't think. Know."

Rule: Use quotation marks for dialogue. Each time a new speaker begins, begin a new paragraph.

> Examples:
>
> "What would you like to bake?" Aunt Felicity asked. Then she waited for your answer.
>
> "I don't know. I guess I'd like to follow one of your favorite recipes," you answered.
>
> "Sugar cookies are my favorite," she replied.

Rule: Use quotation marks to indicate words that are ironic or unfamiliar.

Examples:

When she opened the door to her son's room and saw that it looked as if a tornado had blown through, she had to wonder what he was thinking by saying yes when she asked if the room was now "clean."

The five-year-old, in a French restaurant for the first time, looked to several utensils to the left of his place setting, and with a great sense of "accomplissement," chose the smallest fork with which to pick up a tiny cornichon.

✍ **Tip**

It's best not to overdo emphasizing words. Too much of it makes for "scare quotes," and then you can lose your readers' trust.

Italics are often an alternative to quotation marks for emphasis. Though we occasionally italicize a word that comes from a language other than English, it's good to check your dictionary first. Many words once considered foreign are now a part of everyday English and require no special treatment, not even italics.

Quotation Marks and Other Punctuation Marks

If you've ever looked at the written work of an elementary school kid who's just learning how to use quotation marks (and is writing by hand rather than typing), you've seen two things: overuse of quotation marks (they're fun!) and ambiguous placement of punctuation. When unsure, kids tend to put punctuation marks directly beneath the closing quotation marks. Though many grammar rules are debatable, this one isn't. Marks go either inside or outside.

Inside

Rule: Put a period inside the closing quotation marks.

> Example:

> Psychologist and writer Timothy Leary said, "Think for yourself and question authority."

Rule: Put a comma inside the closing quotation marks.

> Example:

> "Your room is not clean," she said.

Outside

Rule: Put a colon or semicolon outside the quotation marks.

> Example:

> She gave an excellent critique of a new song, "Scooby-Scooby-Scooby-Dooby"; however, I don't believe she's ever listened to it.

Inside or Outside

Rule: Put other punctuation marks inside or outside depending on whether they belong to the quoted material only or to the whole sentence.

> Examples:
>
> Is it possible that you've never heard the song "Moon River"?
>
> She asked pleadingly, "Will you please go see the movie with me?"

 Tip _____

Dialogue has its own conventions. If the attribution (the *he*, *she*, *they*, or *we said*) comes first, we use a comma at the end of the attribution, before the quoted material. If the quoted material comes first, we typically punctuate it with a comma and then end the attribution with a period. But an exclamation point or question mark may be appropriate punctuation for the quoted material:

> Aunt Felicity asked, "Do you like sugar cookies best?"
>
> "They're my favorite," you answered.
>
> "I thought so!" She smiled in reply.

_____

Quotations Within Quotations

Rule: Put single quotation marks around quoted material that appears within quotation marks.

> Example:
>
> "What did you think I meant by 'clean' when I said to clean your room?" she asked.

IN A NUTSHELL

Have you ever watched a beginning reader try to make sense of words on a page? Looking at symbols, processing them, and understanding them as words with meaning is a complicated task.

As readers, we need help organizing and separating the symbols we see so we can recognize and understand words, sentences, and paragraphs.

As writers, it's our job to provide the organization. Capitalization and punctuation are parts of that organization. They guide your readers in two ways.

First, they create conventions we learn to associate with meaning. For example, the White House we understand is a particular building in the capital city of the United States of America, rather than a little white house that's on a country lane.

Second, capitalization and punctuation help us interpret text. For example, they tell us to stop or pause between thoughts, giving us a chance to take in what we've just read. They alert us to different speakers. They let us know when material comes from another source, rather than from the writer of the main text.

You've met lots of rules. There's no way around that. But the more you write and edit, the more easily you'll incorporate the rules into your grammar knowledge base.

Initially, using punctuation and proper capitalization can be like following a long set of driving directions to a new destination. Your first trip might feel like navigating a maze. You'll need to refer to your map frequently. But after you've made the drive a few times, you'll know the directions by heart.

Almost Goodbye...

Editing Checklist and Farewell

In this book, you've been to a dinner party, an all-night diner, a superstore, a cafeteria line, and a fast-food restaurant. You've sampled cookies, mango sorbet, cherry pie, vegetables, veggie burgers, fries, and a smoothie.

Now that you've completed Chapter 12, is there anything else ahead? Yes!

Editing Checklist

There's one more meal before you go: a checklist of editing suggestions. Add to it, take away from it, and shape it to your individual needs to make it a useful personal guide:

✓ Keep a dictionary and your favorite grammar resources by your side. You'll be much more likely to answer your own questions and satisfy your doubts if your reference materials are conveniently nearby.

✓ Take a break between writing and editing. You'll be able to see your work more clearly and objectively. Even under time pressure, try to arrange for a breather. A day is good. Five minutes are better than none.

✓ Edit on your screen *and* edit a printout. On a piece of paper, you might see something you missed on the screen.

✓ Read your work aloud. You might hear what you didn't see.

✓ Read your work aloud to someone else and ask someone to read your work aloud to you. Different voices will bring different things to your attention.

✓ Read your work from the bottom up, sentence by sentence. The unfamiliar sequence may alert you to something you missed.

✓ Use the Learning Goals from the start of the book to make an outline.

✓ Use that outline as a grammar checklist.

✓ Tailor the checklist to your specific needs and check your work against it, point by point.

It's true that there's always more to learn. I hope this book will serve as a resource for you for a long, long time.

Grammar can be tough. Celebrate each new thing you learn! Every small change you make contributes to big improvements in your writing.

FAQs

Q: What's an en dash?

A: An en dash is bigger than a hyphen and smaller than an em dash. We use it to express "through" and "to" in a few situations.

> Examples:
>
> The final vote was 54–67.
>
> Menus specials will be available February 13–15.
>
> Note: Use either words or the en dash, but not a combination:
>
> No to this: The specials will run again at the end of the year, from December 29–31.
>
> Yes to this: The specials will run again at the end of the year, from December 29 to 31.

Q: Do you put periods in the abbreviations for state names?

A: This depends on which style guide you follow. The United States Postal Service provides a period-free list of abbreviations for state names. These are good for addressing envelopes!

Q: Are there any other uses for the colon?

A: Yes. We use the colon for numerical expressions of time, title/subtitle constructions, and biblical references.

> Examples:
>
> 6:59 p.m.
>
> *A History of Punctuation: A Is for Apostrophe*
>
> Jeremiah 18:23

Chapter 12 Quiz

Question 1

Which require capitalization?

    a. people's names, pets' names

    b. seasons, numbers

    c. generic family relations, generic professions

Question 2

Choose the valid comma rule.

    a. Use a comma before a conjunctive adverb that joins two independent clauses.

    b. Use a comma to separate a subject and its verb.

    c. Use a comma before a direct address.

Question 3

Which is a valid use of single quotation marks?

    a. for a quotation within a quotation

    b. for an ironic word

    c. for a very short quotation

Answer Key: Q1:a Q2:c Q3:a

COMPREHENSIVE QUIZ

(a.k.a. Your Final Exam)

Question 1
Which can be a linking verb and an action verb?

- a. think
- b. smell
- c. seem

Question 2
Which are examples of homophones?

- a. sea/see
- b. ugly/hideous
- c. hot/cold

Question 3
Which sentence has a plural possessive?

- a. They hoped to invest three weeks' pay each year.
- b. None of the parents wanted to go on the overnight camping trip.
- c. Everybody's scheduled to attend today's all-hands-on-deck meeting.

Question 4
What is a compound predicate?

- a. a verb phrase
- b. predicates joined with a conjunction
- c. a complex sentence

Question 5

Without this, a sentence fragment will result.

a. prepositional phrase

b. logic

c. predicate

Question 6

You can fix a run-on sentence by doing which of the following?

a. adding punctuation to the end of the sentence

b. rewriting to make all clauses dependent

c. adding punctuation or punctuation plus a conjunction

Question 7

What is a *base form* verb?

a. the starting place for conjugating a verb.

b. the foundation tense for a verb

c. a simple tense verb

Question 8

Which statement explains reflexive pronouns?

a. They add extra intensity.

b. They mirror their subject.

c. They change form from subject to object.

Question 9

Choose the right verb to fill in the blank in this sentence: "Long, close-fitting pants _____ prevent tick bites when you're on a hike."

a. helps

b. help

Question 10

Which example uses parallel structure?

    a. to fulfill your dreams, your desires, fulfill your goal, and fulfill your needs

    b. joining the crowd, experiencing the event, and appreciating the energy

    c. to join the crowd, experiencing the event, and to appreciating the energy

Question 11

Name the grammar problem in the following sentence: "The mystery box was square in shape."

    a. wordiness

    b. logic

    c. ambiguous modifier

Question 12

Which sentence has an ambiguous pronoun problem?

    a. The son asked his father if he could drive to work today to get there on time.

    b. The daughter asked her mother, "Are you going to give me a warning?"

Q12:a	Q6:c
Q11:a	Q5:c
Q10:b	Q4:b
Q9:b	Q3:a
Q8:b	Q2:a
Answer Key: Q7:a	Q1:b

COMPREHENSIVE QUIZ 263

P.S.

I hope you had a great time with this book and that you'll come back to it whenever you want to reinforce what you learned. Some parts of grammar stick; we tend to remember what we use the most. But some parts are tough, and you may have some questions down the road. I'd love it if you wanted to stay in touch!

You can reach me at ellen.sue.feld@gmail.com.

REFERENCES

Everything I've ever learned about grammar—from teachers (elementary school on up), colleagues, books, websites, family, and friends—has contributed to this book. The following references are my go-to grammar bibles. They don't always agree with one another, but they always provide food for thought.

AP Stylebook Online
store.stylebooks.com

The Chicago Manual of Style Online
www.chicagomanualofstyle.org

The Free Dictionary
www.thefreedictionary.com

Merriam-Webster
www.merriam-webster.com

And this one got me started when I didn't know where to begin:

Glazier, Teresa Ferster. *The Least You Should Know about ENGLISH: Basic WRITING Skills: Form C*. New York: Holt, Rinehart, and Winston, 1981.

RESOURCES

There's always more to explore! These wonderful sites will keep you going.

Chapter 1

Dictionary.com
www.dictionary.com
This dictionary draws its definitions from more than one source. An audio icon accompanies many of the entries, so you can listen to pronunciations.

Grammar Revolution
www.english-grammar-revolution.com/parts-of-speech.html
Here you'll find explanations for the eight parts of speech and some handy lists that provide lots of examples. This site also offers sentence diagrams, which can help you see parts of speech in action.

Guide to Grammar & Writing
grammar.ccc.commnet.edu/grammar/prepositions.htm
There's more to prepositions than meets the eye. This comprehensive page will tell you everything you need to know about prepositions ...and more.

Merriam-Webster
www.merriam-webster.com
This dictionary includes an audio feature for many entries. Select the sound icon next to a word when you'd like to hear its pronunciation.

Purdue Online Writing Lab
owl.purdue.edu/owl/general_writing/grammar/articles_a_versus_an.html
If you're not sure whether to use an article in front of a word or how the sound of a word guides the choice of *an* versus *a*, then check this site, where you'll find plenty of explanations and answers.

Chapter 2

Homophone.com
www.homophone.com
Are you looking for more homophones to add to your list? This site offers an expansive, alphabetized list and a nifty feature: Select a word, and you'll be taken directly to its dictionary definition.

TheFreeDictionary.com (Dictionary)
www.thefreedictionary.com/dictionary.htm
If your conventional dictionary doesn't have entries for two-word phrases like *all ready* or *a lot*, visit this site to discover definitions and usage notes.

TheFreeDictionary.com (Idioms)
idioms.thefreedictionary.com
Have you ever wondered if the expression is "rack your brain" or "wrack your brain"? Visit this site to learn about idioms and phrases. You can type in a word and see how it's used in a variety of expressions.

Chapter 3

Apostrophes
www.lynchburg.edu/academics/writing-center/wilmer-
writing-center-online-writing-lab/grammar/apostrophes
This is the apostrophe page of a punctuation page provided by
the University of Lynchburg.

GrammarBook.com
www.grammarbook.com/punctuation/apostro.asp
This is the apostrophe page of Jane Straus's online reference
guide to grammar and punctuation. You'll find lots of
examples here.

Guide to Grammar & Writing
grammar.ccc.commnet.edu/grammar/marks/apostrophe.htm
If you've ever wondered how to make a single letter or number
into a possessive or a year into a plural, you'll learn about those
rules and more on the apostrophe page at this site.

The Learning Center's Online Writing Lab
depts.dyc.edu/learningcenter/owl/exercises/
apostrophes_ex2.htm
In contractions, a misplaced apostrophe results in a spelling
mistake. Give yourself a little extra contraction practice by
trying the exercise here.

Chapter 4

500 Sentence Diagrams
www.german-latin-english.com/diagrams.htm
Do you love diagramming sentences? Spend some time at this
website created by scholar Eugene R. Moutoux. You'll find
everything from simple sentences to lengthy examples from
classic literature.

Diagramming Sentences

grammar.ccc.commnet.edu/grammar/diagrams/diagrams.htm

Diagramming can be a great way to understand sentences, particularly for those who like to learn from concrete visuals.

Subjects and Predicates Multiple-Choice Exercise

highered.mheducation.com/sites/0073123587/student_view0/chapter6/subjects_and_predicates_multiple-choice_exercise.html

This quiz offers more practice identifying subjects and predicates in simple sentences.

The Linking Verb

chompchomp.com/terms/linkingverb.htm

Are you baffled by linking verbs and need more information to be confident in your ability to recognize them as predicates? This online resource will help.

Bonus Resources

There's always more to learn! Words that look like verbs may not be operating as verbs. These resources will tell you about gerunds, participles and infinitives.

owl.purdue.edu/owl/general_writing/mechanics/gerunds_participles_and_infinitives/comparing_gerunds_participles_and_infinitives.html

www.cliffsnotes.com/study-guides/english/verb/verbals-gerunds-infinitives-and-participles

Chapter 5

Sentence Fragments
owl.purdue.edu/owl/general_writing/mechanics/sentence_fragments.html
Here you'll find examples of sentence fragments and suggested ways to correct them.

The Clause
www.chompchomp.com/terms/clause.htm
Learn more about clauses and how to distinguish between dependent and independent clauses.

The Phrase
www.chompchomp.com/terms/phrase.htm
Visit this terrific resource to learn more about phrases and to see examples of phrases in action.

Chapter 6

Comma Splices, Fused Sentences, and Run-ons
leo.stcloudstate.edu/punct/csfsro.html
The presentation of run-ons and corrected sentences on this site can be of particular value to visual learners.

Conjunctions
grammar.ccc.commnet.edu/grammar/conjunctions.htm
If you're not sure which coordinating conjunction is best to join your clauses, the information here will help.

The Coordinating Conjunction
www.chompchomp.com/terms/coordinatingconjunction.htm
Learn more about coordinating conjunctions and when to use them versus subordinating conjunctions.

Chapter 7

Passive Verbs
owl.purdue.edu/owl/general_writing/grammar/verb_tenses/
passive_verbs. html
Most of the time, active voice is best, but sometimes passive
voice is the way to go. (This resource uses the term "passive
verbs.") Here you'll learn effective use of passive voice.

Sequence of Verb Tenses
grammar.ccc.commnet.edu/grammar/sequence.htm
Here you can learn more about verb tenses and proper
sequence of tenses.

Sneaked vs. Snuck
www.merriam-webster.com/video/sneaked-vs-snuck
This video exploration of irregular verb "snuck" will introduce
you to a brief history of regular and irregular verbs in the
English language.

What Is the Subjunctive Mood?
www.grammar-monster.com/glossary/subjunctive_mood.htm
The subjunctive mood can be mystifying. Learn more about it
here and try the quiz.

Chapter 8

HyperGrammar
arts.uottawa.ca/writingcentre/en/hypergrammar/
using-pronouns
This page about pronoun reference and tricky usage is
produced by the Writing Centre at the University of Ottawa.

Merriam-Webster
www.merriam-webster.com/video/the-awkward-case-
of-his-or-her
This short video lesson explains why the word *their* can be a
valid choice when you don't know whether to use *his* or *her*.

Reflexive and Intensive Pronouns
macmillanmh.com/ccssreading/treasures/grade6/ccslh_g6_
lg_8_1d_15.ht ml
This page provides more sentence examples with reflexive and
intensive pronouns.

Chapter 9

Agreement When Words Come Between (Interrupt) the
Noun and Verb
www.esc.edu/online-writing-center/exercise-room/
agreement-when-words-come-between-noun-and-verb
Try this exercise from Empire State College for more practice
with noun-verb agreement.

Pronouns and Pronoun-Antecedent Agreement
grammar.ccc.commnet.edu/grammar/pronouns.htm
This page from the Guide to Grammar & Writing offers a good
review. Note: Not all of the quiz links are working.

Chapter 10

A Match Made in Heaven: Subjects and Predicates
writingcenterunderground.wordpress.com/2014/04/01/a-
match-made-in-heaven-subjects-and-predicates/
This blog piece offers examples of mixed constructions and
does an excellent job explaining them..

Shifty Tenses
www.iup.edu/writingcenter/writing-resources/grammar/tense-shifting
This page on tense shifts offers good examples of when and how to shift verb tense correctly.

The Slot
www.theslot.com/parallel.html
The SHARP POINTS pages are full of intelligent and funny articles. You'll find a good example of, and sharp commentary about, parallel structure.

The Slot
www.theslot.com/jfk.html
Here's yet another informative article about parallel structure from SHARP POINTS.

Chapter 11

Guide to Grammar and Style
jacklynch.net/Writing
From this introductory page, you can link to the sections about audience, split infinitives, and more. You can also use the alphabetical contents to link to other areas of interest, such as *c* for a section on clarity and *d* for sections on dangling modifiers, diction, and dictionaries.

Guide to Grammar & Writing
grammar.ccc.commnet.edu/grammar/confusion.htm
Explore this page to find information about wordiness, confusing modifiers and pronouns, and more.

Wordiness, Wordiness, Wordiness List
web.uvic.ca/~gkblank/wordiness.html
Here you'll find an extensive A-to-Z list of words to reduce or remove from your writing.

The Writing Center, University of Wisconsin-Madison
writing.wisc.edu/handbook/style/css_wordyphrases
Visit this terrific page for a concise presentation of wordy phrases and at-a-glance alternatives.

Chapter 12

Capitalization
www.infoplease.com/ipa/A0001601.html
Here you'll find a concise presentation and examples of rules for capitalization.

Editorial Style Guide
apps.communications.uci.edu/style-guide
Provided by the University of California, Irvine, this alphabetically organized style guide is useful for looking up and discovering the proper way to abbreviate, spell, capitalize, and punctuate everything from acronyms to zip codes.

Bonus: Lists

These pages provide helpful guidelines for presenting and punctuating lists.

www.purchase.edu/editori al-style-guide/general-style-preferences/punctuation/bulleted-and-numbered-lists

getitwriteonline.com/articles/vertical-lists

More About Words
englishmistakeswelcome.com/more%20about%20words.
htm#Writing%20
Get to know more rules for capitalization, how to handle
periods with abbreviations, when to use numerals, and more.

Paradigm Online Writing Assistant
www.powa.org/edit/basic-punctuation
This is the punctuation page of an extensive site. Explore and
you'll find lots of wonderful material about writing.

The Punctuation Guide
www.thepunctuationguide.com/index.html
This nifty guide lets you click on punctuation marks to learn all
about the rules that govern them.

A Quick Guide to Punctuation
www.lynchburg.edu/academics/writing-center/wilmer-
writing-center-online-writing-lab/grammar/a-quick-guide-
to-punctuation
This nifty resource supplies exactly what its title suggests.

ACKNOWLEDGMENTS

To all the marvelous people at Mango, thank you for your professionalism and warmth and for making it fun to make a book! To my agent, the superlative Janelle Rosenfeld, thank you for your smarts and loyalty and for holding my hand tight. To my husband and children—a family of language aficionados— how lucky am I to be able to sweat over commas (and a whole lot more) with all of you? So lucky.

INDEX

ABOUT THE AUTHOR

Ellen's interest in grammar ignited way back in 1980, when she started teaching developmental writing at the College of Staten Island (CUNY). Quickly realizing how much she didn't know, she studied the student textbook, learned and loved the language of grammar, and brought it into play in the classroom. Through the decades, Ellen has worn a variety of editorial hats, including newspaper reporter and copy chief, personal essayist, website reviewer, and developmental editor. She is the creator/instructor of online grammar refresher courses with more than 45,000 enrolled learners, the author of the children's storybook *Paragon and Jubilee*, and the inventor/maker of a humane dog-training harness. As a dedicated vegan, Ellen uses no animal products in the many food-based grammar examples you'll find in this book.

Photo by Jo Rosen
Photography/Johanna Resnick Rosen

ABOUT THE AUTHOR